THE ABOLITIONISTS

Immediatism and the
Question of Means

Problems in American Civilization

UNDER THE EDITORIAL DIRECTION OF *George Rogers Taylor*

THE ABOLITIONISTS

Immediatism and the Question of Means

EDITED WITH AN INTRODUCTION BY

Hugh Hawkins

AMHERST COLLEGE

Problems in American Civilization

D. C. HEATH AND COMPANY: Boston

INTRODUCTION

A<small>T</small> the time of the American Revolution, thoughtful patriots recognized the inconsistency of holding Negroes as slaves while justifying revolution on grounds of man's inalienable natural right to liberty. By 1804 all the original states north of Maryland and Delaware had taken legal action to end slavery within their borders. In some cases the abolition was immediate, in others gradual. (As late as 1860 the census reported a few slaves in New Jersey.) States in the South, where Negroes were more numerous and where the invention of the cotton gin shortly made plantation slavery profitable over wide areas, did not adopt a policy of abolition. But there as in the North, small groups, often led by Quakers, organized to oppose the institution of property in man.

Although some of these state and local antislavery societies dated from Revolutionary times, the American Colonization Society, organized in 1817, was the first national society for furthering emancipation. Led by men of social standing in the upper South and aided by the federal government in establishing Liberia, the society proposed to colonize free Negroes in Africa and thus to increase voluntary manumissions. But by 1865 the society had transported only a few thousand Negroes while the number in the country had grown to over five million.

The 1830s saw a revolt against the gradualist program of this society. New journals and societies made "immediate abolition" their program. The most conspicuous journal, *The Liberator*, was launched in 1831 by William Lloyd Garrison, an impecunious Massachusetts printer recently associated with the colonizationist editor Benjamin Lundy. The largest organization, the American Anti-Slavery Society, was formed in 1833; it had been originally planned by a group of New Yorkers including Arthur and Lewis Tappan, wealthy merchant supporters of revivalist Charles G. Finney. Garrison wrote the society's Declaration of Sentiments and changed his own New England Anti-Slavery Society into its Massachusetts branch.

The reasons for the emergence of a new sort of abolitionism in the 1830s are still very much matters for historical debate. But certain factors were clearly important. Parliament ended slavery in the British West Indies in 1833, and this victory for British antislavery forces followed a shift of their demand from gradual to immediate emancipation. Such evangelical leaders as Finney increasingly emphasized human responsibility in resisting sin, and the application to slavery seemed clear and compelling to some. Meanwhile, disillusionment set in for many who observed the ineffectiveness of colonization and grew suspicious of its rationale, which emphasized the dangers from free Negroes as much as the evils of slavery. In a period of vigorous reform activity the drunkard, the prisoner, the lunatic, the debtor, the child, the woman, and the workman were all becoming objects of concern, and their treatment by society was sharply questioned. It would have been strange if amid this ferment the predicament of the slave had been ignored.

There was a decided ambiguity in the term "immediate abolition." Garrison apologized for ever having supported the "pernicious doctrine of gradual abolition" and advocated uncompensated, unconditional, universal emancipation at once; nevertheless, he admitted that slavery would not be "overthrown by a single blow," though "it ought to be." The New York City Anti-Slavery Society, led by the Tappans, also attacked the "delusive dream of gradual abolition" and praised the British doctrine of immediatism, but the society interpreted as immediate such action as was promptly commenced and gradually accomplished. The program of the national society avoided particular plans for abolition, acceptance of the principle being considered the important thing. There were indications, however, that such gradualist procedures as advancing slaves to freedom through stages of peonage or apprenticeship would be acceptable. As far as the public was concerned, such qualifications had little effect. The phrase "immediate abolition" was taken at face value. Indeed, by 1838, deeply impressed by reports of the success of the reform in the West Indies, leaders of the national society declared their position to be an unqualified immediatism without "the perplexing processes of gradualism."

American reform efforts are notoriously given to internal bickering and the splintering off of dissidents. Immediatists, having broken from the colonizationists, continued to undergo division. In 1839, the decision to make the issue distinctly political by organizing a third party split the movement. The next year Garrison took over as president of the national organization, and those favoring political action (and disapproving Garrison and his eagerness to mix other reforms with abolitionism) withdrew to form the American and Foreign Anti-Slavery Society. Neither national organization ever recaptured the vigor of the mid-1830s. Abolitionist activity centered thenceforth in the various state societies

and in the Liberty Party. The latter merged with the Free Soil Party in 1848, thus supporting a "weaker" position of much stronger public appeal—prevention of the spread of slavery.

In spite of these vicissitudes, there was never so distinct a break between Garrison and other immediatists as there had been between colonizationists and immediatists. It is true that Garrison's tendencies toward freethinking and anarchism set him and his closest followers apart from the majority of immediatists, who engaged in revivalistic preaching services and in efforts to obtain governmental action. But there was a broad area of means which Garrison and almost all other immediatists shared: the appeal to public opinion, the use of an emotional vocabulary, the unremitting exposure of slavery at its worst, and the invocation of "higher law." In a word, the immediatists made agitation their principal method. For this they have been damned and defended from their day to ours, and the damning and defending have—justifiably—been applied broadly to the whole movement.

Beyond agitation lay the possibility of physical assault upon those who held slaves. Nothing seemed further from the intentions of early immediatists. The Declaration of Sentiments of 1833 announced to the world: "[Our principles] forbid the doing of evil that good may come, and lead us to reject, and to entreat the oppressed to reject, the use of all carnal weapons for deliverance from bondage; relying solely upon those which are spiritual, and mighty through God. . . . [Our measures] shall be such only as the opposition of moral purity to moral corruption—the destruction of error by the potency of truth—the overthrow of prejudice by the power of love —and the abolition of slavery by the spirit of repentance." The Declaration contrasted this renunciation of violence with the means used by the Founding Fathers, who in the American Revolution had been willing "to spill human blood like water, in order to be free." Among the immediatists some came to believe that what was right for the fathers was right for the sons. From an initial position that justified a fugitive slave in resisting recapture, some moved ever further toward belief in a war for liberation. The abolitionist John Brown turned to physical force in the 1850s. Whether he had done right or wrong was a painful but inescapable question for other immediatists. Lewis Tappan, asking Virginia's governor to pardon Brown, repeated the movement's early rejection of "carnal weapons." Garrison declared himself still a "peace man," but to the question "Was John Brown justified in his attempt?" he answered, "Yes, if Washington was in his." Wendell Phillips pronounced John Brown "the impersonation of God's order and God's law, moulding a better future, and setting for it an example." In embracing Brown as a martyred hero of their cause, the abolitionists involved themselves deeply in any judgment that is passed on the means he chose.

The central concern in this volume is not the merits of antislavery and proslavery arguments, but rather the methods adopted by those opponents of slavery who from the 1830s on pressed for its immediate abolition. These readings touch only occasionally on political activity, though many abolitionists consciously chose that as a means. The necessary compromises and appeals for wide voter support tended to prevent antislavery politicians from becoming or remaining immediatists.

The readings that follow begin with two selections published respectively in 1948 and 1939 by two historians whose interpretations of the abolitionists of a century earlier reveal sharp differences of emphasis. With this background of information and interpretation, the student next encounters a series of documents written by abolitionists and their critics between 1831 and 1852. These have been selected from occasions when the methods of the abolitionists rather than the merits of slavery were up for consideration. John Brown, whose activities constitute a separate but related problem, is the protagonist in Part III. Here two able historians take passionately different stands on the Harpers Ferry Raid. A final section comprises three attempts to make such concepts of the social and behavioral sciences as social status, personality, and institutional development relevant to historical judgments of the abolitionists. With the help of these analyses the student can refine his own evaluation of abolitionist methods. Perhaps too he can find ways in which the nature of abolitionism reveals the nature of American society.

The undercurrent of emotion in the writings of historians represented in this collection indicates that abolitionists are investigated not only because they are historically significant, but also because historians find them relevant to their own social values. This is understandable. Slavery has been abolished, but full equality for Negroes in American life has not yet been attained. If those who support this goal hope to profit from the experience of abolitionists, they cannot allow them to remain unexamined heroes or villains.

The problem of means which abolitionists raised seems particularly apropos for today's reformers dealing with matters of race. But for any who feel concern over shortcomings in American life, there are insights to be obtained by "rethinking the thoughts" of supporters and critics of abolitionist measures. Does forthright denunciation change those whose social customs are being criticized, or does it rigidify them? When, if ever, is one's own conscience adequate justification for the violation of man-made law? When, if ever, can one condone or practice violence in opposition to a social evil? Such questions were debated over one hundred years ago when immediate abolitionists sought and gained public attention. Their example deserves study by those who must answer such questions today.

CONTENTS

CONTENTS

The Clash of Issues

An immediate abolitionist of the 1830s defines her position and defends agitation on the slavery issue:

> If our fundamental principle is right, that no man can rightfully hold his fellow man as *property*, then it follows, of course, that he is bound *immediately* to cease holding him as such. . . . Every slaveholder is bound to cease to do evil *now*, to emancipate his slaves *now.* . . .
> "Much evidence," thou sayest, "can be brought to prove that the character and measures of the Abolition Society are not either peaceful or christian in tendency, but that they are in their nature calculated to generate party spirit, denunciation, recrimination, and angry passion." . . . The truth is, the efforts of abolitionists have stirred up the *very same spirit* which the efforts of *all thorough-going* reformers have ever done; we consider it a certain proof that the truths we utter are sharper than any two edged sword, and that they are doing the work of conviction in the hearts of our enemies.
>
> —Angelina Grimké

But at the same time a theologian challenges the means of such opponents of slavery:

> It is not by argument that the abolitionists have produced the present unhappy excitement. Argument has not been the characteristic of their publications. Denunciations of slaveholding, as man-stealing, robbery, piracy, and worse than murder; consequent vituperation of slaveholders as knowingly guilty of the worst of crimes; passionate appeals to the feelings of the inhabitants of the northern States; gross exaggeration of the moral and physical condition of the slaves, have formed the staple of their addresses to the public. . . . There is in this conduct such a strange want of adaptation of the means to the end which they profess to have in view, as to stagger the faith of most persons in the sincerity of their professions, who do not consider the extremes to which even good men may be carried, when they allow one subject to take exclusive possession of their minds.
>
> —Charles Hodge

By 1852, a leading abolitionist claims that results have justified the approach of immediate abolitionists:

> To have elaborated for the nation the only plan of redemption, pointed out the only exodus from this "sea of troubles," is much. This we claim to have done in our motto of Immediate, Unconditional Emancipation on the Soil. The closer any statesmanlike mind looks into the question, the more favor our plan finds with it.
>
> —Wendell Phillips

Of abolitionists' attitude toward John Brown's raid, one historian, who agrees with their judgment, writes:

To those who regarded slavery as "the sum of all villainies," as legalized kidnapping maintained by jails, the lash, and, ultimately, the death penalty for those who sought to secure their freedom or to help others do so, Brown's action was one of great idealism and placed him in the company of the great liberators of mankind.

—LOUIS RUCHAMES

Another historian, who condemns abolitionists' involvement in the Harpers Ferry episode, issues this warning:

While the hateful violence of today's Southern mobs is condemned, the violence of Brown and his supporters is viewed as humanitarian activism. The present concern for civil rights has helped to obscure the historical case against Brown and to obscure what it means to glorify the Harpers Ferry Raid.

—TILDEN G. EDELSTEIN

One scholar raises doubts about both the motives and the methods of abolitionists:

Perpetual reformers, though resented as meddlers by those they disturbed, have been hailed as pioneers and martyrs who have unselfishly helped to usher in new eras and a better world.

The modern psychologist is somewhat skeptical of such explanations. He talks of youthful experiences, maladjustments, inferiority complexes, and repressed desires. He is not so sure about the sources of the reform impulse or the unselfish character of the reformer. The student of social affairs is likewise less inclined to grant unstinted praise to the fanatic and is not certain about the value of the contribution.

—AVERY CRAVEN

However, another suggests why historians may now reach a more favorable judgment:

Out of their heightened concern with the pressing question of Negro rights, a number of historians, especially the younger ones, have begun to take a new look at the abolitionists, men who in their own day were involved in a similar movement of social change. About both them and ourselves we are asking anew such questions as the proper role of agitation, the underlying motives of both reformers and resistants, and the useful limits of outside interference. From this questioning a general tendency has developed to view the abolitionists in a more favorable light than previously.

—MARTIN B. DUBERMAN

I. HISTORICAL INTERPRETATIONS OF THE ABOLITIONISTS

Charles S. Sydnor: PROLOGUE TO THE END OF SLAVERY

Significantly, one of the best brief accounts of the rise of immediate abolitionism appears in a volume in the series A History of the South. *The rapid spread of plantation slavery through the lower South helped stimulate abolitionist activities and these activities in turn encouraged sectional self-consciousness among Southerners. In the following chapter from* The Development of Southern Sectionalism, 1819–1848, *the late Charles S. Sydnor surveys the varieties of abolitionist strategy and the mounting Southern resentment and fear. A native of Georgia, Sydnor's other writings include* Slavery in Mississippi *and* Gentlemen Freeholders: Political Practices in Washington's Virginia. *Before his death in 1954, he taught for many years at Duke University.*

THE issues that troubled the 1820's were nearly all quieted by the end of the nullification controversy. The Missouri Compromise had settled the question of slavery in the territories of the United States. The westward removal of the Indians left little ground for future quarrels between Southern governors and the nation over questions of Indian policy. Jackson's attitude toward internal improvements, particularly his veto of the Maysville Road Bill, brought to a close the series of arguments over the propriety of using Federal funds to supply the transportation needs of the nation. Likewise, his veto of the bill to recharter the national bank indicated that it would be fruitless for Congress to attempt to pass another such bill as long as he was President. As for the tariff, the measure that was passed in 1833 set forth a nine-year program, and there

was a general agreement on both sides of the fence to respect this settlement. The doctrine of nullification had failed to gain substantial support outside the state of its origin, and there was no reason to think that the nation would soon be disturbed by its resurrection.

With these issues settled, most of them permanently, the rising tide of Southern sectionalism might have been expected to recede after 1833 just as New England sectionalism had ebbed after the War of 1812. But this was not to be. At the very time when the old issues were being quieted, the slavery question was entering a new and more disturbing phase.

In the fall of 1829 a pamphlet was discovered in the hands of blacks at Savannah, Georgia, entitled *Walker's Appeal, in Four Articles, together with a Preamble to the Colored Citizens of*

From Charles S. Sydnor, *The Development of Southern Sectionalism, 1819–1848,* pp. 222–226, 229–244, 247–248. Volume V of *A History of the South.* Copyright 1948 by Louisiana State University Press. Reprinted with permission. For footnotes see the original.

the World, but in Particular, and Very Expressly to Those of the United States of America. Its author, David Walker, was a free-born Negro of Wilmington, North Carolina, who had recently moved to Boston and opened a shop for selling old clothes. The *Appeal* was published in Boston in September, 1829.

The essential points in the *Appeal* were that American Negroes had been reduced to the *"most wretched, degraded,* and *abject* set of beings that *ever lived* since the world began"; that slaveholders were exceedingly oppressive and cruel; that slaves were capable of attaining freedom by destroying their masters; and that it was their duty as men and as Christians to do so. Walker declared that white men would "take vessel loads of men, women and children, and in cold blood, and through devilishness, throw them into the sea, and murder them in all kinds of ways." He regretted that black men had not fought for their lives. He warned: "Get the blacks started, and if you do not have a gang of tigers and lions to deal with, I am a deceiver . . . let twelve black men get well armed for battle, and they will kill and put to flight fifty whites." He gave the stern counsel: "If you commence, make sure work—do not trifle, for they will not trifle with you—they want us for their slaves, and think nothing of murdering us in order to subject us to that wretched condition—therefore, if there is an *attempt* made by us, kill or be killed."

Within a few months copies of this pamphlet were found in Virginia, North Carolina, South Carolina, and Louisiana as well as additional copies in Georgia. Its discovery caused great excitement. State legislatures—sometimes in secret session—passed laws to keep the slaves from getting possession of writings that

might cause unrest or revolution. Georgia and North Carolina, copying the example of South Carolina at the time of the Denmark Vesey insurrection, passed laws to quarantine incoming Negro seamen. Prohibitions were laid, or if already in existence were made more stringent, upon teaching slaves to read and write. North Carolina free Negroes were prohibited from peddling wares outside the counties in which they resided and from leaving the state and returning at will.

Although the discovery of the *Appeal* put the ruling class of the South on the alert and made laws governing black men more severe, little if any hostility was engendered toward the North, for the revolutionary doctrines preached by Walker met with strong Northern disapproval.

Before the excitement aroused by the Walker pamphlet had subsided, the press began to carry reports of a great debate in the British Parliament in August, 1830, over the abolition of slavery in the colonies. News that the British were bringing slavery to an end disturbed the planting states; on the other hand, this news stirred American opponents of slavery to more vigorous action and to more radical proposals. One of the individuals who was greatly influenced by the British debate was the twenty-four-year-old William Lloyd Garrison, who was then in Baltimore assisting Benjamin Lundy with the publication of his *Genius of Universal Emancipation*. On the first day of the following year he was in Boston bringing out the first issue of the *Liberator*.

In the second issue, Garrison distinguished between his own program and that advocated in the *Appeal*. "We deprecate," so he wrote, "the spirit and tendency of this Appeal. . . . *We* do not preach rebellion—no, but submission and peace." Although Garrison appealed to conscience rather than to physical force, the violence of his invective, his distortion of facts, and the savagery of his indiscriminate attacks upon all slaveholders seemed more likely to lead to emotional and violent action than to a reasonable and peaceful solution. Furthermore, his demand for immediate action without regard to consequences, his bitter denunciation of all laws that gave a legal basis for slavery, including the Constitution of the United States, and his opposition to the use of political action left scarcely any way of settlement except by physical force. At times, the *Liberator* advocated action in this realm. On July 23, 1831, it published a "Song, Supposed to be Sung by Slaves in Insurrection," urging them to "strike for God and vengeance now." The following month a body of slaves struck in Southampton County, Virginia, under the leadership of Nat Turner.

Turner was born in Southampton County in the year 1800. His mother was a native African, and she brought him at an early age to believe that he possessed supernatural powers. As he grew to manhood he claimed that he could hear voices directing him, read signs in the heavens, and remember events that had transpired before his birth. By these and other means he gained considerable leadership among his fellow slaves. His influence was strengthened and extended to neighboring plantations by his being a Baptist preacher. Not much is known as to the motives behind his crime. Inasmuch as he later asserted that his master had treated him well, they cannot be explained on the ground of personal abuse. Neither was it ever proved that he had been influenced by Garrison or by the *Appeal*, although this was suspected because he had been taught to read by his master's son. But it is clear that he had been planning for several years before he finally struck, and according to his account he was pushed onward in his course by voices, visions, and an eclipse of the sun.

A singular blueness in the atmosphere in August, 1831, convinced Turner that the time had come. At a secluded spot in the woods he met with four confederates and two neophytes. With a barbecued pig for food and brandy for refreshment and stimulant, they laid plans. One of the new recruits had good reason for hating his owner, but Turner chose the home of his own master, Joseph Travis, as the place to begin. Striking before dawn on Monday, August 22, Turner and his followers slaughtered Travis' family. From then until the following morning they moved from plantation to plantation, killing between fifty and sixty persons without regard to age or sex. Nearly half were children, and more women than men were killed. Bodies were mutilated, and Turner sprinkled his followers with the blood of the dead. As he moved forward, he augmented his force by coercion as well as by persuasion. Estimates of its size have varied all the way from forty to two hundred.

On Tuesday morning the roles of hunter and hunted were reversed when a party of white men overtook, attacked, and scattered the band. Military units were soon scouring the countryside, and self-constituted patrols joined in the hunt. Some of them matched the brutality of Turner, torturing and killing innocent Negroes as well as guilty ones. Fifty-three Negroes were arrested and brought to trial. Of these, twenty-one were acquitted. Among the last was Turner who had eluded his pursuers more than two months—long after all the others had been killed or captured.

The outbreak in Southampton County turned the thoughts of men in other parts of the South to the danger of similar disasters. The fact that Turner had been taught to read, that he had exercised the influence of a preacher, and that he might have been stirred by the writings of Walker or Garrison suggested that laws be passed to bind the minds and restrict the activities of slaves. Vigorous attempts were made to force free Negroes to leave the South. There were many commentators who believed, however, that the chief need was for better law enforcement rather than for new laws. And there were some, especially in Virginia, who were convinced that the root of the trouble was neither in imperfect legislation nor inadequate enforcement, but in the fact that slavery was injurious to society and was dangerous, and that the danger increased as the ratio of slaves to whites increased. . . .

Northern opinion had little effect upon the genesis or the course of the Virginia slavery debate [of 1831–1832], but while this debate was in progress a movement was developing in the North that was soon to have tremendous influence upon the South. It began as a religious revival in upstate New York in the middle 1820's under the leadership of Charles G. Finney, an eloquent and powerful preacher, who exhorted Christians to *"aim at being useful in the highest degree possible"* by working for temperance, education, and the reformation of society. His phenomenal success rested partly on his power to enlist young men, imbue them with his own fervor, and send them out to carry on the work. His ablest recruit was Theodore Dwight Weld, who by 1830 was the most powerful agent in the West for the American Temperance Society.

Sweeping over the West, Finney's revival reached its crest in the year 1830, with converts being won by the tens and hundreds of thousands; and at the crest Finney invaded New York City. The event was significant, for it brought the powerful religious impulse of the revival movement into close contact with a group of charitable and reformatory societies. Among their objectives were the distribution of Bibles and tracts, the establishment of Sunday schools, the advancement of education, the promotion of Christian missions, the salvation of sailors, and the attainment of temperance, prison reform, and peace among the nations. These organizations were then called benevolent societies, and New York was in some measure the capital of the benevolent empire. Most of the societies held their conventions each May in New York, and that city was the home of a small group of men who furnished the active leadership for most of these national societies. Chief of these men were Arthur and Lewis Tappan, wealthy New York merchants.

The Tappans welcomed Finney. To help him overcome opposition in New York and to assure him moral and financial support, they organized some of their business friends into an Association of Gentlemen. Thus there was formed a powerful alliance of religious fervor, reformatory zeal, organizational experience, and economic power.

This alliance was turned toward the abolition of slavery chiefly by the example and the propaganda of British antislavery forces. The British benevolent societies had been the models and inspiration of most of the American societies; and in 1831, while the question of slavery in the colonies was coming to a crisis in England, the Association of Gentlemen decided to establish an American antislavery society. However, they postponed action until they could take advantage of the high tide of interest which they expected America to feel when Parliament should take its final step against slavery.

When that time came, the Gentlemen hesitated; but they were forced to go ahead by Garrison, who was enjoying temporary prestige and power by having been feted and applauded in England as the self-appointed ambassador of American abolitionists. In December, 1833, the American Anti-Slavery Society was organized at Philadelphia. Although Garrison's influence in the Society was to be short-lived, his prominence in the meeting that created it invested the young organization with something of his reputation for fanaticism. Besides this unfortunate occurrence, the Society did itself great injury by making confused statements of its purpose. It advocated immediate emancipation, but it hastened to explain that this term did not mean what an ordinary man would think it meant; rather it meant immediate emancipation gradually accomplished.

During the first year of its life the Society aroused Northern hostility toward abolitionists rather than toward slaveholders, and this hostility was strong enough to subject abolitionists to various forms of physical violence. To overcome these handicaps, the leaders of the Society tried to convince the public that Garrison was not the leader or the spokesman of their organization, and they strove without success to silence him. But though 1834 was a year of discouragements, it contained one event that was soon to turn the tide. The theological students at Lane Seminary at Cincinnati, many of whom were con-

verts of Finney, considered the question of abolition in what was called a debate but was in reality more of a protracted revival meeting. Weld, who was one of their number, was mainly responsible for the wholesale transformation of this group of able young men into ardent abolitionists.

The Lane debate caused a great stir. President Lyman Beecher and the trustees sought to repress the abolition activities of the students. Instead, they drove them away to become the nucleus of Oberlin College. In the years 1835 and 1836, thirty of these young men were among the most effective of the missionaries of abolition. With the spirit of zealots and martyrs they endured "harsh words . . . stale eggs, and brick-bats and tar," but they won a hearing. They "precipitated another Great Revival in the nation, a revival in abolition."

Weld was notably courageous and successful. When he entered a new community he usually met with all manner of indignities. While speaking before one audience, he was hit in the face by an egg. Before another, a large stone, hurled through the church window, struck him in the head and stunned him for several minutes. He earned the title of being "the most mobbed man in the United States." But he kept going, usually for many nights in succession; and his calm spirit, his winsome personality, and his fervent eloquence often transformed enemies into abolitionists. By the end of 1835, he had planted the seed widely in Ohio. The next year he worked in Pennsylvania and New York State. Meanwhile, Garrison was keeping up the agitation in New England, antagonizing the clergy and other powerful groups, but winning some converts, notably Wendell Phillips, who respected Garrison for "the austerity of his life and his singleness of purpose." Others, like William Ellery Channing, opposed slavery while remaining aloof from the activities of the American Anti-Slavery Society.

But it was the Society which gave form and much of the driving force to the abolition movement. In 1835 it issued a great stream of pamphlets and newspapers, most of which were given away and mailed in bundles to those who might be disposed to distribute them. In June it was planning to "issue gratuitously from 20,000 to 50,000 of some publication or other every week." The mailpouch invasion of the South came to grief in South Carolina. Citizens of Charleston, learning that a considerable quantity of abolition literature was in the post office awaiting distribution, forcibly seized the offensive publications and burned them on the Parade Ground. The New York postmaster, acting on the suggestion of Postmaster General Amos Kendall, announced that he would forward no more antislavery matter to Southern addresses. This event, together with the enactment in most of the Southern states of laws making the circulation of abolition literature a felony, effectively closed the South to the pamphlet campaign of the Society.

Even in the North, the results of the pamphlet campaign were discouraging, and in 1836 the Society decided to shift its emphasis and resources back to the approach which had earlier proved more effective, namely, the use of zealous agents. Enough new recruits, "men of the most unquenchable enthusiasm and the most obstinate constancy," were carefully trained, and added to "Weld's ardent host" to bring their number up to the New Testament number of seventy. Almost all were theological students or clergymen. A full measure of

fervor and devotion was needed, for the abolition doctrine was still detested throughout most of the North. However, a development in Congress in the winter of 1835–1836 began to turn the tide, and the Society was quick to take advantage.

In the Congress that assembled in December, 1835, there was a sharp increase in the number of petitions praying for the abolition of slavery and of the slave trade in the District of Columbia. At the time, it was well understood that there were probably no more than one Representative and one Senator willing to vote for a change in the status of slavery in the District. Nevertheless, Congressmen who did not favor such legislation continued to present petitions. The explanation for this curious situation lies chiefly in the political situation. Jackson was President, and his party controlled the House. The members of the newly formed Whig party, seeking in every way possible to discredit and obstruct the Democrats, soon struck on the presentation of abolition petitions as an effective instrument to sow dissension between Northern and Southern Democrats and to consume much time that the Democrats needed for carrying out the party's program. Whigs presented more than 95 per cent of the petitions that were brought to the House.

Southern Congressmen were stung to the quick by the phrasing of some of the petitions which referred to slavery as "the foul stain of legalized plunder" and to slaveholders as "the villainous enslavers of souls." On December 18, 1835, James H. Hammond of South Carolina exclaimed that: "He could not sit there and see the rights of the southern people assaulted day after day, by the ignorant fanatics from whom these memorials proceed."

In an atmosphere of party conflict complicated by sectional feeling, much of the winter was spent by the Whigs in plaguing the Democrats with abolition petitions, and by the Democrats in trying to find a way to extricate themselves without running counter to the constitutional right of petition. It may be that the problem was insoluble, but both houses of Congress attempted to find a solution. The rule followed in the Senate was less objectionable and aroused less controversy than the rule adopted in the lower house.

On May 25–26, 1836, the House, after acrimonious discussion, resolved that Congress had no authority to interfere with slavery in the states and that it ought not to interfere with slavery in the District of Columbia; that it was important to end agitation on the subject so as to restore tranquillity to the public mind; and that "all petitions, memorials, resolutions, propositions, or papers, relating in any way, or to any extent whatever, to the subject of slavery, or the abolition of slavery, shall, without being either printed or referred, be laid upon the table, and that no further action whatever shall be had thereon. It should be noted that there was little difference between this rule and the previous custom in the House of laying such petitions upon the table after they were presented.

This rule, commonly known as the gag rule, utterly failed to end agitation. Former President John Quincy Adams was now a member of the House of Representatives. He characterized himself as the friend of "universal emancipation," and as the possessor of antislavery views so extreme that "the sturdiest of the abolitionists would have disavowed" them. Adams took up the gauntlet with the solemn declaration: "I hold the resolution to be a direct violation of the constitution of the United States, the rules of this House, and the rights of my constituents."

The question of whether the fateful resolution was in fact unconstitutional has been variously answered by subsequent students. At the time, some abolitionists believed that the logic of the argument permitted them to go no farther than to brand the rule as a "virtual" denial of the right of petition. But constitutional refinements were beyond the understanding of most men. The Northern public, overlooking the party issues at stake, accepted the half-truth that defenders of slavery stood opposed to the right of petition and that slaveholders were willing to subvert the Constitution to maintain their evil institution.

The American Anti-Slavery Society made it its business to keep abolition petitions pouring into Congress. It printed and sent them out by the millions, asking the abolition of the slave trade between the states, the abolition of slavery in the territories, and praying that Arkansas and Florida be denied admission to the Union as slave states. With lists of signatures pasted on, these petitions came back to Congress by the hundreds of thousands. More than 99 per cent of the petitions were printed. Between December, 1837, and April, 1838, enough of them were presented to Congress to fill "a room $20 \times 30 \times 14$ feet, close packed to the ceiling."

The Whigs, who had made such effective use of petitions to sabotage the Democratic administration, came into power in the election of 1840. Throwing consistency to the winds, they enacted gag resolutions more stringent than those against which they had been complaining. Even Adams for the moment forgot the constitutional scruples that had disturbed him, and through him the North; for he remarked that he could "not deny the right of the House to refuse to receive a petition when it is first presented."

Both parties were in some measure now committed to the non-reception of antislavery petitions, and the controversy over the right of petition largely ceased. But during the years it raged, it enabled abolitionists to make Congress their sounding board and to compel even slaveholders to help the cause of abolition. Southern Congressmen, goaded into angry remarks, had fanned the fire that they wanted to extinguish. As one of the abolitionists sagely remarked: "Slaveholders are prime agitators." The gag rule had put the South in an extremely bad light. And it had enhanced the prestige of the abolitionists. Instead of appearing as pious and meddlesome fanatics, they now appeared as the champions of a great constitutional right.

During the petition controversy, Weld prepared two books that were to have tremendous influence in the abolition crusade. One was designed to show the horrors of slavery; the other, to prove that emancipation would be followed by an agreeable state of affairs. Using material collected by two abolitionists who had been sent to the British West Indies, Weld edited so plausible a study of the satisfactory effects of emancipation that the leaders of the American Anti-Slavery Society abandoned the complex formula of immediate emancipation gradually accomplished and announced that henceforth their goal was immediate abolition. The general public, whether hostile or friendly, had always believed that this was the object of the Society.

The other study, entitled *American*

Slavery as It Is: Testimony of a Thousand Witnesses, was essentially a case study in the worst features of slavery. Weld, with the help of research assistants, combed thousands of Southern and other newspapers for atrocity stories, and he appealed to abolitionists to supply him with "facts never yet published, facts that would thrill the land with horror." Within four months, 22,000 copies of his powerful indictment of slavery had been sold, and within the first year, nearly 100,000. The influence of *American Slavery as It Is* went far beyond its many readers, for it was an easily accessible store of ammunition for subsequent campaigners. A large part of Charles Dickens' influential chapter on slavery in his *American Notes* was lifted bodily and without any expression of indebtedness from Weld's compilation, and its service to Harriet Beecher Stowe in the preparation of *Uncle Tom's Cabin* was frankly acknowledged.

At the end of the 1830's there occurred an important change in the management and the character of the abolition movement. The American Anti-Slavery Society was torn by quarrels among its leaders, and the Panic of 1837 brought these men and their organization to virtual bankruptcy. State societies revolted against the parent organization, and the women's-rights movement caused distraction and confusion of purpose. But as the New York leadership declined, the empire that it had largely created found a new capital in Washington and a leadership in a small group of Congressmen, assisted by a lobby of their creation.

For a time these Congressmen were prohibited from speaking against slavery by the rule of silence that both parties adopted in the effort to avoid rifts within their ranks. When Thomas Morris, a Democratic Senator from Ohio, challenged this rule and spoke against Calhoun's 1837 resolutions he was refused re-election by the Democratic legislature of his state. Early in 1842, Adams, probably with the approval of the small but well-knit group of abolitionist Representatives, threw down the gauntlet to the Whig party with a bitter and powerful attack upon slavery. A caucus of Southern Whigs decided that he should be censured. Northern Whigs concurred. But when the attempt was made, Adams won a notable victory on the floor though, so it was rumored, at the price of promising to remain silent in the future.

Shortly afterward, the abolitionists commissioned Joshua R. Giddings, an Ohio Whig, to issue another challenge by speaking against slavery. He did so and was censured. Thereupon he resigned his seat, appealed to his constituency, and was re-elected by a large majority. Back in Congress, he resumed his attack upon slavery, and the Whig leaders knew that they could not stop him; for in the fight in Ohio over his re-election, the forces of abolition had proved stronger than the power of the Whig organization. The day had dawned when the Whig party could not forbid discussion of this issue even though its discussion was likely to rend the party into Southern and Northern factions. Abolitionists could now look to Congressmen to give them leadership and to speak and vote for their cause.

This great turning point is a convenient moment for reviewing certain developments in the antislavery movement during the previous decade. In sheer numbers, its growth was phenomenal. Its respectability and influence had likewise increased. Instead of being scorned and stoned in Northern villages, aboli-

tionists now had a great following among respectable folk, and they had vigorous leaders in Congress.

In respect to their goal, the abolitionists were singularly consistent throughout the years. Although they had abandoned the idea of gradualism, they never swerved from their essential goal of extinguishing slavery throughout the United States at the earliest possible date. Neither had they ever assumed responsibility for suggesting how to cushion the shock of emancipation or how to deal with the problems that would follow it. On the other hand, their strategy was somewhat codified. At first the abolitionists appealed both to Southerners and Northerners; but when the South barricaded itself against printed appeals and condemnations, the program of the abolitionists became primarily an attempt to convince Northerners, who neither owned slaves nor posessed the legal power to abolish slavery, that slavery was terrible and ought to be ended. An occasional abolitionist was worried by the impractical character of their approach. One of them implored Weld to supply him with "a plain common Sense view of . . . *how* emancipation and abolition are to be brought about by the correction of public sentiment at the North. . . . Can you not furnish . . . some *facts* pertinent to . . . the *effectiveness* of Northern abolition on the South?" But most of the antislavery men, like the majority of the other reformers of their day, showed less zeal for reforming sinners than for persuading the righteous to denounce sinners.

In the early days of the movement there were debates among abolitionists as to whether slavery was an evil or a sin; but the doctrine soon gained general acceptance among them that human bondage was contrary to the will of God.

From this decision there flowed several important consequences. The slavery debate was turned into Biblical channels, with both sides in the controversy searching the Scriptures for proof that their views were in accordance with the revealed will of God. A second consequence was the condemnation of the slaveowner as a sinner; and while such a man as Finney thought the sinner ought to be reproved in a spirit of love and humility, the doctrine of the sinfulness of slavery led to a censorious attitude toward the slaveholder.

The doctrine that slavery was a sin was a natural outgrowth of the religious origin of the abolition movement. It was also natural that as the religious impulse diminished, as it did in time, the fight against slavery should lose some of its lofty, spiritual tone. Francis Wayland, president of Brown University and a strong opponent of slavery, agreed with "the late lamented Dr. [William E.] Channing, in the opinion that the tone of the abolitionists at the north has been frequently, I fear I must say generally, 'fierce, bitter, and abusive.'" It was, thought Wayland, "very different from the spirit of Christ." Finney, watching the course of events, was much disturbed, fearing lest abolition without a foundation of sincere and genuine Christianity would bring the nation "fast into a civil war."

But Weld was not fearful. At times he seemed to long for the appearance of "a storm blast with God in the midst." If slaveholders had refused to heed his warnings and reproofs, which he was sure were the warnings and reproofs of God, was it not inevitable and proper for them to be destroyed by insurrection and war? Some twenty years earlier John Quincy Adams had looked upon disunion and civil war as sublime and glorious if for the purpose of ending slavery, and there is much to indicate that his mind was still filled with these thoughts during his great fight for the right of petition in Congress.

In spite of all that has been written about the abolition crusade, no one can tell with certainty how much it accelerated the ending of slavery in America, whether civil war could have been avoided without it, or whether in the long run it made the problem of race more or less acute. To take a broader sweep, no one can prove beyond question that the South, or the nation, or the Negro's status in America was made better or worse by the activities of the abolitionists. But on less important points, some of which bear upon these larger questions, something can be said about the effects of the abolition movement.

As for the slave, his lot was not much changed; certainly it was not improved. A thoughtful Scotch minister, who was no friend of slavery, came to the opinion after extended travel in America in 1844 that "Nowhere does the condition of the coloured people appear worse than in the slave States which border the free States. . . . Whatever may be the ultimate advantages, the immediate effect of the agitation for emancipation, and all the anxious, uncertain, suspicious, and angry feelings it engenders, is unfavorable to the improvement either of master or slave, making one more suspicious, and the other the more deeply to feel his chain." The free Negro population of the South also suffered. In Maryland and Virginia, where the number had been increasing more rapidly than the number of slaves until there were more than 100,000 free Negroes in 1830, the rate of increase was thereafter sharply cut. In Louisiana and Mississippi there was an absolute decrease between 1840 and 1850.

Travelers in the South began to find that they were objects of suspicion. The Reverend George Lewis was asked soon after he arrived at Savannah in the year 1844: "Are you come to be a spy here?" Before entering Virginia in 1837 a British naturalist, Charles B. B. Daubeny, took the precaution of disposing of some antislavery writings that had been in his traveling bag. The experiences of the prominent English Quaker, Joseph J. Gurney, illustrate the behavior and the treatment of the abolitionist in the South. In Virginia he freely stated his "views respecting the oppressed negro population" to Governor David Campbell. Although Gurney felt that he was kindly received, he recorded that Campbell "bitterly complained of what he called the violence of the Northern abolitionists" and asserted "that their proceedings had operated, in Virginia, as an effectual bar to the progress of emancipation." In Charleston he asked Mayor Henry L. Pinckney to convene some of the principal persons of the city to hear his story of the favorable workings of freedom in the West Indies, but Pinckney thought it would be imprudent. On the other hand, Gurney was given free access to whatever he wished to inspect, including the jail, the Negro prison, and a plantation on Edisto Island. He left the city with the opinion that "we had certainly been received with much more kindness and polite attention, than we had ventured to expect."

Slave traders in the neighborhood of Washington must have become accustomed to sight-seers and to persons collecting data on the evils of slavery, and they seem to have shown them about with an easy tolerance. Planters occasionally submitted their estates to examination even at the risk of having to listen to private lectures on the evils of slavery or of having their visitors seek to create unrest among the slaves.

But it was not the occasional visitor who disturbed the Southerner so much as the incessant attack in Northern press and pulpit and upon the floor of Congress. Despite the religious impulse behind the barrage of advice, warning and denunciation, the slaveholder failed to see therein much evidence of the Christian virtues of truth, humility, and love. He was impressed, rather, by the holier-than-thou spirit of his mentors, a spirit which seemed to imply that Northern consciences were more enlightened than any to be found in the South.

Undoubtedly, the slaveholder did not give the abolitionists a fair hearing. His traditions, his economic interests, and his way of life all fought against his considering slavery in a detached, objective fashion; and his dealings with the North for some years past had destroyed any faith he may have had in Northern disinterestedness and fair dealing. As he looked to the region that was now inviting him to perform a costly and revolutionary act, he remembered that the opposition of this region to the extension of slavery in 1819 had been blended with a plan to increase New England's political power. As he recounted the contests in subsequent years over protective tariffs, over the expenditure of Federal funds for roads and canals, and over other issues, he could recall little but self-interest, and at times a very ruthless self-interest, in the words and votes of Northern Congressmen.

Perhaps slaveholders should have distinguished between such men as Weld and Finney, who fought slavery because they considered it morally wrong, and Northern politicians, who voted for measures that would enhance Northern prosperity even at the expense of the South. But slaveholders failed to make that distinction; and after 1840, when the abolition movement entered politics with the formation of a bloc of antislavery Congressmen, the distinction largely ceased to exist.

As Southern opinion hardened toward abolitionists, Southern criticism of slavery waned. By the year 1837 there was not an antislavery society in all the South. "In the general indignation," excited by abolitionists, wrote George Tucker of Virginia in 1843, "the arguments in favour of negro emancipation, once open and urgent, have been completely silenced, and its advocates among the slaveholders, who have not changed their sentiments, find it prudent to conceal them." The careers of politicians were scrutinized to discover whether they were safe on this point. James McDowell, Jr., an antislavery spokesman during the Virginia debate over slavery, had his record flung against him when the legislature was considering him for the governorship in 1840; and although one of his friends assured the legislature that McDowell was hostile to Northern abolitionists, he failed of election at this time.

The effect of abolitionism on Southern opinion is illustrated by the official statements of two Mississippi governors. In 1828, Gerard C. Brandon declared that slavery was "an evil at best" because it was harmful to the poor white man, it widened the gulf between rich and poor, and it kept the state from attracting a numerous white population and from enjoying the influence and power that such a population would bring. Eight years later John A. Quitman, after reviewing and condemning the rise of the abolition movement, stated before the legislature: "It is enough, that we, the people of Mississippi, professing to be actuated by as high regard for the precepts of religion and morality, as the citizens of other states, and claiming to be more competent judges of our own substantial interests, have chosen to adopt into our political system, and still choose to retain, the institution of domestic slavery."

This was the sort of calm but determined statement proper in official messages, but it does not reflect the surging emotion aroused in the South. Southern hotheads threatened to lynch abolitionists if they came south of the Potomac River and offered rewards of thousands of dollars to anyone who would put them in reach of Southern vengeance. A Mississippi newspaper declared that the quarrel over slavery had reached such a point that it would "not be settled by negotiation, but by the *sword*,—by balls and the *Bayonet. We can do without the North.*"

Although the abolition movement was followed by a decline of antislavery sentiment in the South, it must be remembered that in all the long years before that movement began no part of the South had made substantial progress toward ending slavery. The free and full discussion in Virginia in 1832 was promising, but the decision was in the negative. The trends are not clear enough to warrant prophecy as to what the South would have done about slavery had it not been disturbed by the abolitionists, but it is at least certain that before the crusade began Southern liberalism had not ended slavery in any state.

The Southern defense of slavery antedated the organization of the American Anti-Slavery Society. Shortly after the discovery of the Denmark Vesey plot at Charleston, Richard Furman, president of the Baptist State Convention, published a Scriptural defense of slavery together with a plea for better religious care of slaves. Dew and Leigh defended slavery against the attacks made upon it in the Virginia debate. Under the scourging of the abolition attacks, these defenses were much expanded and new arguments were evolved. To offset the harshly distorted descriptions of abolitionists, southern champions depicted slavery as a kindly and altogether beneficial institution. They turned the pages of history, they dissected human cadavers, and they diligently searched the Bible for arguments to prove that the Negro was made for slavery and that slavery served a useful purpose in society.

The intellectual defense of slavery failed to convert the North—it failed as completely as the abolitionists had failed to convince the South that slavery was sinful. One is tempted to believe that the appeal to reason was in this instance worse than a failure, for instead of bringing the problem nearer to solution, it served merely to convince each contestant of its own righteousness and of its opponent's wickedness, and to stir emotions for an ultimate contest in which reason would play little part. . . .

Even though the constitutional right of the individual state to retain slavery were respected, slavery would be mortally wounded if slaves could not be sold from state to state, if slavery were abolished in the territories and in the District of Columbia, if no new slave states were admitted, and if the powers delegated to the national government—such as the power to tax and to distribute mail—were directed toward injuring slavery.

Dwight L. Dumond: THE ABOLITION INDICTMENT OF SLAVERY

In the 1930s the publications of Dwight L. Dumond and Gilbert H. Barnes reshaped the history of abolitionism. These two Midwestern scholars emphasized the significance of their region and of evangelical religion in the rise of immediate abolitionism. They also deflated earlier views of William Lloyd Garrison's importance in the movement. The following portion of Dumond's Antislavery Origins of the Civil War in the United States, *typical of this revised view, gives an intimate account of the activities in Ohio and Kentucky of Theodore D. Weld and James G. Birney. At the time he gave the lectures from which the following passages come, Dumond had edited Southern editorials on secession, the letters of Birney, and (with Barnes) the letters of Weld, Angelina Grimké Weld, and Sarah Grimké. In 1961 he published his monumental* Antislavery: The Crusade for Freedom in America. *The fruit of many years' research, the book revealed an even stronger sympathy for abolitionism than the lectures here represented. Dumond teaches at the University of Michigan.*

ON September 15, 1834, James G. Birney and Theodore D. Weld met at a farmhouse twenty miles north of Georgetown, Kentucky. They had come on horseback, one from Danville, the other from Cincinnati, exercising care to prevent recognition and to preserve the utmost secrecy in their deliberations. Two years before Weld had been entertained at Birney's home in Huntsville, Alabama. Now, he feared to be seen with Birney in Kentucky lest his presence should add to the already heavy burden of opposition Birney was seeking to overcome. This was a day of confirmation. Both men had passed from hope to skepticism and then to outright disbelief in the efficacy of colonization. They had published their convictions; had pledged anew their faith in abolition; and had met again to plan the course of future action. Neither man yet knew the full measure of sacrifice it would entail, nor is it likely either cared.

Birney had always lived in solid comfort, if not in luxury. His father was a wealthy trader and rope manufacturer of Louisville. His relatives, his friends, and his professional associates all were members of the Southern aristocracy. He himself had been a slaveholding planter and prominent attorney in Huntsville. He had served in Alabama's first constitutional convention and had been intimately connected with the founding of its university. Had he remained in Alabama and loyal to his class, he would undoubtedly have risen to high position in public service. He was a man of indomitable courage and unyielding conviction, a devoted husband and father, an old-school Presbyterian, and a Whig

Reprinted from *Antislavery Origins of the Civil War in the United States* by Dwight L. Dumond (pp. 21–48, 88–92) by permission of the University of Michigan Press, Copyright © by the University of Michigan, 1939. For footnotes see the original.

of the landed-gentry vintage. Irish by birth, a humanitarian by instinct, a lawyer by training, he recognized no institutional authority of church, political party, or social caste to modify or to restrain one's individual responsibility to the celestial fire of conscience.

Weld was born in Connecticut and reared in western New York, the son of a conservative, small-town pastor. His formal education was meager, his learning prodigious, his powers of reasoning superb. While yet a young man he went about the western country lecturing upon manual laborism, the science of mnemonics, temperance and moral reform—an itinerant Socrates, with unkempt hair and beard and the simplest attire, caring only for personal cleanliness and the souls of men. He wrote of himself as "an untamed spirit, wild as the winds," stern, contemptuous of opposition, and "proud as Lucifer," "too proud to be *ambitious,* too proud to seek applause, too proud to tolerate it when lavished on me . . . too proud to *betray* emotions, too proud ever for an instant to loose my self possession whatever the peril, too proud ever to move a hair for personal interest, too proud ever to defend my character when assailed or my motives when impeached, too proud ever to *wince* even when the hot iron enters my soul and passes through it." Gifted with rare powers of analysis and persuasion, a natural leader of men, he radiated his influence into every sphere of social reform. He was, in fact, the nerve center of the antislavery movement until the schism of 1840.

We do not know the precise date at which either man began to look askance at slavery, but it was early enough for them to have discussed the subject at length when Weld visited Huntsville in the spring of 1832. Birney's interest arose

from personal knowledge of the sordid aspects of the institution, concern for the future of his young sons, an intense patriotism that saw in slavery a cancerous growth within the body politic, and the common fear that Negro concentration would overwhelm the lower South. It was sufficiently well known for the Colonization Society to offer him the general agency for the southwestern states on June 12, 1832. Weld was the protégé of Charles Stuart, who financed his education, interested him in the slavery question, and was the one living man to whom he bared his heart and made obeisance; but their early association was as members of Charles Grandison Finney's band of revivalists, and Weld's fame as an orator was established before Stuart himself turned to the question of slavery. Weld's trip in 1832 was in behalf of Oneida Institute and manual laborism particularly, and of a prospective theological seminary incidentally. As early as March, 1830, Stuart had been writing to interest Weld in slavery; Weld joined with Tappan, Jocelyn, Goodell, and others in a discussion of the subject in 1831; and he turned aside on his journey in 1831–32 to indoctrinate the faculty at Western Reserve College, including Beriah Green, Elizur Wright, and President George Storrs; but in what? In opposition to slavery, of course, though certainly not in hostility to colonization and an endorsement of immediate emancipation of slaves to be retained and elevated among their former masters, because he wrote to Birney in September, 1832, from Cincinnati: "When I look at the great slave question, trace its innumerable and illimitable bearings upon the weal of the world, every year augmenting its difficulties, its dangers, its woe and its guilt, my heart aches with hope deffered [*sic*], mocks all prescriptions and refuses to be comforted. I am ripe in the conviction that if the Colonization Society does not dissipate the horror of darkness which overhangs the southern country, we are undone. Light breaks *in from no other quarter*."

Birney, in the interim, had abandoned his legal practice and for one year strove mightily to convert the Southwest to the cause of colonization. Like Weld, he was opposed to slavery, but an immediate emancipationist could hardly have written: "If the abolitionist be really desirous of benefitting his fellowmen, and of advancing the cause of human happiness . . . we would invite him to visit those parts of the *South*, where there is, already, a large proportion of the free colored class. If he be diligent, judicious and dispassionate, we risk nothing in saying, that he will be convinced of the superior wisdom of trying every other plan, bearing upon its face the least appearance of feasibility, before experiment be made of his favorite *Abolition*."

The point I wish to make is that, to say a man was opposed to slavery means very little except that he was not a devotee of the positive-good argument. There was a vast difference between antislavery and abolition. The tests of abolitionism were: (1) willingness by those who owned no slaves to bring about a state of emancipation by compulsion; (2) refusal to countenance expatriation; and (3) insistence upon according to the emancipated slaves all the privileges and civil liberties of free men. Neither Weld nor Birney was an abolitionist in the summer of 1832, though they were to play the stellar rôles in the great human drama of the next decade.

The two years between these conferences—July 1832, and September, 1834 —was a preparatory period for the complete acceptance of abolition doctrine, a

period in which they were convinced: (1) that colonization was impracticable; that its moving impulse was race prejudice; that it was strengthening rather than weakening the institution of slavery; that it was economically unsound and morally wrong; (2) that slaveholders would never voluntarily enter upon a program even of gradual emancipation; and (3) that the display of intolerance which greeted the mildest discussion of the subject lifted the controversy from the realm of specific reform in a particular section and presaged another episode in the ageless struggle for human rights. Would that the historian might somehow recover the emotions which surge through men's hearts and alter civilizations! It was only a short decade from the day that Birney turned his attention to colonization until he was nominated for the presidency by the Liberty Party, but it was a decade replete with as choice a repertoire of human drama as the nation has ever produced.

Birney's work as agent for the Colonization Society need not detain us long. Its tangible results were negligible: the organization of a few scattered auxiliary societies, the launching of a small parcel of emigrants on the steamer *Ajax* from New Orleans, the publication of a series of fifteen essays on the subject, the delivery of many lectures to mere handfuls of listeners. He discovered a total lack of interest in the subject on the part of both Negroes and whites. Few came to hear him lecture. Newspapers were reluctant to publish his expositions, and only the first seven were reprinted in the official organ of the parent society. Friends implored him to abandon a hopeless cause. Finally, he admitted failure, resigned his agency, severed old friendships, and in September, 1833, sought the hoped-for congenial atmosphere of Danville, Kentucky, scene of his childhood days. On December 11, 1833, he expressed the opinion in a letter to R. R. Gurley, general secretary of the American Colonization Society, that slavery was "altogether un-Christian"; that it would ruin the country unless speedily abolished; and that it was futile to expect its elimination through colonization. Gurley replied to Birney with an amazingly prophetic letter, saying in part: "I deeply regret that there should exist so much apathy, indeed may I not say error of opinion, on the subject of slavery at the South. . . . My own opinion is, that the South must, if its own dearest interests are to be preserved, if the Union is to last, act with vastly more zeal and energy on this subject than has yet been manifested. . . . I hope all this may be done. But I have many fears it will not be effectually done. . . . If it be once understood that the South designs to *perpetuate* Slavery, the whole North will be speedily organized into Anti-Slavery Societies, and the whole land will be flooded with anti-slavery publications."

Almost at the time these letters were written—early December, 1833—a number of gentlemen near Danville formed the Kentucky Society for the Gradual Relief of the State from Slavery, pledging themselves to emancipate all slaves born thereafter when they reached the age of twenty-five years. The Address of the Society signed by John Green, but almost certainly written by Birney, contains some surprisingly advanced doctrine. Of slavery it said: "The sentence of condemnation has been passed upon it by the *Civilized World;* and we venture the opinion that no respectable person will be found in our State, to arraign the decision." The introduction of slavery and its continuance were de-

nounced as "violations of the law of nature," but the latter was the greater wrong because of our "enjoying the full blaze of that light which our own revolution and other similar events have thrown upon the principles of civil and religious liberty—by us who hold up our institutions as patterns from which the statesmen and patriots of other nations are invited to copy, and who boast our country to be the freest on the Globe, and an asylum for the oppressed of every other."

The fundamental principle of the association was stated to be: "That domestic slavery, as it exists under the laws and constitution of this state—perpetual and absolute,—is a great moral and political evil; and that its continuance cannot be justified, before God, the world, or our own consciences, any longer than is necessary to bring it to a termination, less injurious to the parties, than slavery itself."

Repudiating general emancipation without previous preparation as a "wild experiment—endangering the peace and security of the whites, and the very existence of the colored race," it presented the Society's program as "*immediate* preparation for *future* emancipation," justifying it on the ground "that *adequate preparation* for that kind of future gradual emancipation, which will operate beneficially to both the master and slave, can be successfully *commenced* in no other way, than by deciding *first, that slavery shall cease to exist —absolutely, unconditionally, and irrevocably.* When that is settled, then, and not till then, *the whole community* [of whites] *will feel a common interest, in making the best possible preparation for the event.*"

On December 4 there was organized at Philadelphia the American Anti-

Slavery Society, whose doctrine was immediate emancipation, defined as gradual emancipation immediately begun. Professor Gilbert H. Barnes has interpreted this straitened use of the term as an effort to bring British precedent to the movement's support and as realization by its sponsors of the difficulty of applying imperial methods in a country whose general government was one of distinctly limited and delegated powers. Without denying the validity of that interpretation, may I venture to assert that the eastern men were probably no further advanced in their opinions than the Kentuckians, though less gifted with clarity of expression. I have never seen a more crystal-clear statement of what the antislavery leaders of the next ten years were trying to accomplish than the Kentucky statement of the indispensable prerequisite of any program: the decision *"first, that slavery shall cease to exist—absolutely, unconditionally, and irrevocably."*

Before leaving Alabama Birney had abandoned hope for the redemption of the lower South and all his life felt that that region eventually would be overwhelmed by Negroes and abandoned by the whites. He urged Gurley to concentrate all efforts on Kentucky, Virginia, and Maryland, holding that the slave power would collapse and the Union be saved if these states could be induced to get rid of their slaves. He labored indefatigably during the winter of 1833–34 to win his own state to a program of gradual emancipation, lecturing at Frankfort, Louisville, and Lexington with Judge John Green and President John Young of Centre College. Many others, including Professor James Buchanan, President Luke Munsell of the Danville Deaf and Dumb Asylum, the Reverend David Nelson of the Danville

Presbyterian Church, and Dr. David Bell, lent their moral support and personal influence. The effort was unavailing, though little organized opposition was encountered, and Birney took the final step of repudiating both colonization and gradualism. Meanwhile events of far-reaching import had occurred at Cincinnati. The students of Lane Seminary, gathered from all parts of the country, were making history under the guiding genius of Weld.

Cincinnati contained more than one-third of the seventy-five hundred Negroes in the state of Ohio, many of whom were emancipated slaves who had been or were then paying for themselves or for their friends or relatives still in bondage. No other place in the United States offered a better opportunity to test the ability of the Negro to make advancement if given the opportunity. Into this mass of humanity these students had thrown themselves without restraint and had established Sabbath schools, day and evening schools, a lyceum where they lectured four evenings a week on grammar, geography, arithmetic, natural philosophy, etc. They mingled freely with the Negro population, relieving distress and cultivating intellectual and moral progress, and incidentally furnishing an excuse for the revival of mob violence. They organized a college lyceum and discussed at length the question of slavery in all its aspects, with particular emphasis upon colonization and emancipation. Colonization was repudiated as unworthy of the support and patronage of Christians, and immediate emancipation was endorsed. There then ensued the first and one of the greatest contests for academic freedom in the history of the country.

The students had given a practical demonstration in refutation of the prevailing belief that Negroes were inherently incapable of advancement and destined by nature to a position of inferiority. They had pooled their intimate knowledge of slavery gained by long residence in the slave states, had reasoned and rationalized as became gentlemen trained in the school of the Great Revival, and had concluded that slavery was a sin great enough to justify their undivided attention.

Thirty members of this theological class were over twenty-six years of age, fourteen were over twenty-eight, and nine were between thirty and thirty-five. All were college graduates, most of them having received degrees from eight to seventeen years previously. Six were married men. One was a practicing physician, and twelve had been public lecturers of prominence. They had come to Lane Seminary perfectly cognizant of the strategic location of the institution. J. L. Tracy, a former schoolmate of Weld at Oneida Institute, then teaching at Lexington, Kentucky, had written to Weld, November 24, 1831: "You are well aware of the fact that this western country is soon to be a mighty giant that shall wield not only the destinies of our own country but of the world. 'Tis yet a babe. Why not then come and take it in the feebleness of its infancy and give a right direction to its powers, that when it grows up to its full stature we may bless God that it has such an influence?" The students themselves declared: "The Valley was our expected field; and we assembled here, that we might the more accurately learn its character, catch the spirit of its gigantic enterprise, grow up in its genius, appreciate its peculiar wants, and be thus qualified by practical skill, no less than by theological erudition, to wield the weapons of truth."

Here in Cincinnati, the most strategic location in the United States, was a new theological seminary with as fine a body of young men as any school in the country, as proved by testimony of their president and by their later accomplishments, and with the possibility of becoming the center of the intellectual and cultural life of the entire valley. Yet all but two or three of the faculty and trustees were so blinded by race prejudice, so devoted to the cause of colonization, so sensitive to popular clamor, and so destitute of knowledge about the true purpose of the educational process as to proscribe the right of free discussion. The students were commanded to discontinue their antislavery society and prohibited from holding meetings and from discussing the subject even at the dinner table. A committee was vested with discretionary power of dismissal. Almost the entire student body requested honorable dismissal. The faculty granted it, but thereafter threw every possible obstacle in the way of the work they were seeking to accomplish. Filled with the glorious vigor of youth, the fervor of religious conviction, and the enthusiasm of the crusader in a worthy cause, the rebels redoubled their efforts among the Negro population, pursued their studies independently, and, finally, went to Oberlin College, where Asa Mahan served as president and Finney came to head theology. But, leaving, they hurled defiance at the faculty in words that stand out as one of the greatest prophecies of the century:

"Sirs, you have mistaken alike the cause, the age and the men, if you think to intimidate by threats, or to silence by clamor, or shame by sneers, or put down by authority, or discourage by opposition, or appal by danger, those who have put their hands to this work. . . . Slavery, with its robbery of body and soul from birth to death, its exactions of toil unrecompensed, its sunderings of kindred, its frantic orgies of lust, its intellect levelled with dust, its baptisms of blood, and its legacy of damning horrors to the eternity of the spirit—Slavery, in this land of liberty and light . . . its days are numbered and well-nigh finished. . . . The nation is shaking off its slumbers to sleep no more."

Meanwhile, Birney, within four months of the date of launching the Kentucky Society for the Gradual Relief of the State from Slavery, became convinced, as he says, that slavery was sinful, although only a hairsplitting divine could explain how a man who had spoken of slavery as unchristian, morally wrong, and a greater evil than original enslavement needed to be convinced that slavery was a sin. What is probably more nearly the truth was Birney's conviction that only through an appeal to the conscience of the slaveholder by preaching the sin of slavery could anything be gained. Early in May, 1834, before the students dispersed for vacation, and previous to the faculty action proscribing academic freedom, Birney wrote his famous "Letter on Colonization, Addressed to the Rev. Thornton J. Mills, Corresponding Secretary of the Kentucky Colonization Society," and followed it shortly with his "Letter to the Ministers and Elders on the Sin of Holding Slaves, and the Duty of Immediate Emancipation." The first was published in the Lexington *Intelligencer*, the second in the Cincinnati *Journal*, and thousands of copies were mailed by the students to ministers and prominent laymen in the Mississippi Valley. They were promptly reprinted in the New York *Evangelist* and the *Emancipator*, and as separate pamphlets by the American Anti-Slavery Society.

Birney and Weld were in constant communication during the summer months (1834). Birney decided to abandon everything else and to devote his life to antislavery work. Arrangements were made for his support by the national society, and it was agreed that he remain in Kentucky, organize a state antislavery society, and establish an antislavery newspaper. He was to labor with the Presbyterian synod of the state to secure antislavery resolutions. Weld was to circle through Ohio and Pennsylvania to Pittsburgh and attend the general assembly there, make arrangements for the organization of an Ohio antislavery society, secure subscriptions to Birney's paper, and return by way of Marietta and Steubenville. The conference near Georgetown in September put the finishing touches to these plans.

During the winter months the Lane rebels trekked to Oberlin, and Weld blazed a trail of abolitionism across Ohio and Pennsylvania. Birney quietly went about his task in Kentucky, organizing the state antislavery society at Danville on March 18, 1835, with James Buchanan as president and Luke Munsell as secretary, publishing a prospectus of his proposed paper—the *Philanthropist*— and making arrangements for printing at the office of the *Olive Branch* in Danville. Then the storm broke.

Thirty-three gentlemen of standing addressed to Birney, on July 12, 1835, a sharp remonstrance against the publication of his paper. Deprecating the failure of the legislature to have laws against such incendiary publications passed—whether from the feeling that none so base could be found in Kentucky society or from the belief that the Negroes were too illiterate to cause concern, or from a desire to preserve the freedom of the press—they requested that Birney forbear until legislation could be secured which would prevent his publication and thus obviate the necessity of resort to mob violence. Birney's reply was a denial of legislative power to interfere with the constitutional guarantee of freedom of the press; a defense of the value of discussion concerning matters of great moment to the people; an assertion that discussion had already begun, would continue, and would be dangerous to the peace of society only if forced underground, concealed, and surreptitiously carried on; and a warning that silence in the slave states would increase discussion in the free states.

Both communications were published in the *Olive Branch*, and the slaveholders, firm in their position that "no *American Slaveholding Community* has found itself able to bear" the experiment of free discussion, called a public meeting at the Baptist Church on July 25. James Barbour, president of the Branch Bank of Kentucky and treasurer of Centre College, presided. The Reverend J. K. Burch, moderator of the Presbyterian synod of Kentucky, was a principal speaker. The meeting, probably of five hundred, left no doubt of its determination to resort to mob violence if necessary to prevent publication of the *Philanthropist*, and passed a series of resolutions denouncing it as a scheme "wild, visionary, impracticable, unpolitical, and contrary to the spirit of our laws, and at war with the spirit of our Constitution." Four days later a mob assembled to destroy the press, but dispersed when its former owner, a member of their own party, took possession of the establishment.

That day marked the end of the organized antislavery movement in Kentucky. Within a month Birney moved his family to Cincinnati. The Reverend David Nelson published a blistering farewell sermon to his congregation and moved to Marion College, Missouri, but was forced to seek safety for himself and family at Carlinville, Illinois. Professor Buchanan accepted a professorship at Oberlin, remained a term, and then also went to Carlinville. Here they joined with the Reverend Robert Holman, Birney's old friend of Huntsville, Alabama, Elijah Lovejoy, and Edward Beecher in founding the Illinois Anti-Slavery Society. Luke Munsell moved to Indianapolis, assisted in organizing the Indiana State Anti-Slavery Society, and became its first president. Of the little coterie only President Young remained, in his heart an abolitionist, openly supporting gradualism, secretly keeping up his contact with Birney.

As for the Lane rebels, it would be difficult to overestimate the influence of these two years. They served as agents of the American Anti-Slavery Society in 1836, abolitionized Ohio, and then formed the nucleus of the famous "Seventy." Henry B. Stanton was financial and corresponding secretary of the American Anti-Slavery Society, an active member of the Free Soil Party, and editor of the New York *Sun*. Asa Mahan became successively president of Oberlin College, Cleveland University, and Adrian College. James A. Thome taught for many years at Oberlin, wrote, with Horace Kimball, the powerful tract *Emancipation in the West Indies,* and served influential pastorates in Cleveland and at Mount Vernon. Philemon Bliss entered Congress from Elyria, Ohio, became chief justice of Dakota Territory and dean of the Law School of the University of Missouri. George Whipple became professor of mathematics at Oberlin, secretary of the American Missionary Association, and a participant in the

Freedman's Aid. Augustus Wattles spent a fortune and the best years of his life teaching free Negroes to become economically self-sufficient, and edited the *Herald of Freedom* in Kansas during that territory's troublous years. Marius Robinson founded and edited until 1861 the *Anti-Slavery Bugle* at Salem, Ohio, and then became president of the Ohio Mutual Fire Insurance Company. Hiram Wilson directed for many years the work of rehabilitation of fugitive slaves in Canada. Hiram Foote, Edward Weed, Calvin Waterbury, John W. Alvord, William T. Allen, and others held prominent pastorates in the West after the agency phase of the movement had been supplanted by political agitation. Professor Calvin Stowe, who "came right" on the question within a few months after the Lane debate, married Harriet Beecher, moved to far-off Andover, and from the recollections of these stirring days came *Uncle Tom's Cabin.*

Judged only by the training of these early apostles of freedom, the events of the two years at Danville and Cincinnati would merit the attention of historians. More important still, they gave character and direction to the movement, making it a powerful religious crusade in the direction of moral reform. It was theological students in a theological seminary, drawing their inspiration largely from the Great Revival, who sat in judgment on the institution of slavery. Weld and Stanton selected the "Seventy" and rarely departed from type in the selection of agents. From first to last churches were the forums, preachers the most consistent and powerful advocates, and the sin of slavery the cardinal thesis of the new social philosophy. The religious character of the antislavery meetings, the Christian piety, meekness, and humility of the pioneer abolition lecturers,

the religious fanaticism which soon enshrouded the entire movement, the particular instructions of the central committee to agents in the field to "insist principally on the *sin of slavery,* because our main hope is in the consciences of men, and it requires little logic to prove that it is always safe to do right," and the intimate notes from one to another, every line of which is a prayer in itself, leave no doubt as to the true character of the first phases of the movement. Birney's emphasis upon the incompatibility of slavery and the fundamental philosophy on which the nation was established blossomed eventually, through his leadership, as the principle upon which Northern sectionalism sought to administer the government.

Finally, the exile of Birney, the very soul of dignity, integrity, and Christian virtue, from his native state and the proscription of academic freedom at Lane Seminary established precedents and enthroned a principle: the slaveholders' interests were paramount and their fiat was law. Birney's perspective was never clearer than when he wrote to Gerrit Smith: "It is as much as all the patriotism in our country can do, to keep alive the spirit of liberty in the *free states.* The contest is becoming—has become—one, not alone of freedom for the *black,* but of freedom for the *white.* It has now became absolutely necessary, that slavery should cease in order that freedom may be preserved to any portion of our land. The antagonist principles of liberty and slavery have been roused into action and one or the other must be victorious. There will be no cessation of the strife until Slavery shall be exterminated or liberty destroyed."

No other reform movement is quite like the antislavery crusade, because it was based upon an appeal to the con-sciences of men; yet the sinners were al-most wholly insulated from the preach-ment, and the anxious seat was crowded with saints, so that the historian is tempted to agree with Pascal, that "There are but two classes of men, the righteous, who think themselves to be sinners, and the sinners, who think themselves right-eous." One *expects* to find the contem-porary literature of the great controversy strongly biased, but race prejudice still lives, and the writings of trained his-torians, also, have such an overtone of moralizing or apology as to leave the im-pression their wishes determined what they should accept as truth. Fortunately, we do not need to agree on the precise nature of American Negro slavery. His-torians have too long focused their atten-tion upon that controversial point, to the neglect of more important things. One can no more describe the life of the slave than describe a typical plantation. There was too much diversity, and the human element entered in too largely to per-mit even a highly centralized picture. To attempt it is to become lost in a labyrinth of qualifications. Abolitionists omitted the qualifications and strength-ened their case accordingly, but weak-ened it in the light of historical re-search.

One may find in abolition literature, not here and there but in dreary succes-sion, charges of vilest depravity: mis-cegenation between owners, owners' sons, and overseers—whom Birney called the "feculum" of society—and the female slaves, with all the accompanying trage-dies of mixed blood, sale of children by their fathers, pollution of men's souls and degradation of the home; slave breeding, ranging from the encourage-ment of promiscuity and inducements for continuous bearing of children, to

compulsory submission to service by Ne-groes and whites of fine physique and degenerate character; separation of fam-ilies, of husbands and wives, brothers and sisters, and children of tender age from mothers, either from financial stringency, liquidation of estates, or downright disregard of human feelings; virtual freedom to comely young fe-males willing to prostitute themselves and share their earnings; mutilation of bodies, in anger, in search of punishment equal to the nature of the offense, or in satisfaction of sadistic impulses; brand-ing, shackling, placing in stocks, burden-ing with iron collars, chains, etc., to pre-vent running away; criminal neglect of the injured, the seriously ill, and the in-curably diseased for the sake of econ-omy; and the merciless hunting down of fugitives with bloodhounds and guns, with the levity and zest of the possum hunt.

The weakness of this sort of propa-ganda lay in the necessity (1) for a con-stant increase in the enormity of the of-fense charged; (2) for variation, since attention was more easily arrested by the novelty of the guilt than by its degree; and (3) for unimpeachable supporting evidence to satisfy the skeptic. Some of the pornographic calendar is so stereo-typed in form as to bear the impress of legend. Some of it was hearsay, un-doubtedly magnified in the telling. The more repulsive incidents were of uncom-mon occurrence and were no more au-thentic criteria by which to judge the in-stitution as a whole than was Jefferson Davis' experiment in self-government for his slaves. It was the sort of stuff that warms the heart of the true propandist and fascinates the sanctimonious pietist as well as the irreligious miscreant. But such aspects of slavery as miscegenation, separation of families, cruel punishments, and barbarous treatment of fugitives cannot be minimized either by one who seeks a true picture of slavery or by one who seeks the causes of the Civil War. Historians have no justification for ignoring abolition literature in their work on slavery. The great bulk of this part of it was written by high-minded men and women who were either born and reared in the South or had lived there many years. One would hardly expect to find mention of these sordid aspects of the institution in plantation records, in private diaries or letters, or in treatises written in defense of slavery. The fact that Southerners who did write about them were living at the time in states where there was no slavery does not detract from, but rather increases, the probability of their accuracy. Supported, as they were, by certain other indisputable facts we shall shortly refer to, they would have given all but the most obdurate champions of slavery cause for serious reflection; but the generality of Southerners had not the slightest conception of abolition arguments or of the principles for which they were contending.

The restlessness of slaveholders over colonization activities crystallized into a militant defense of slavery as antislavery agitation increased in the North— a defense which denied freedom of speech and of the press, excluded abolition literature from the mails, and drove everyone suspected of heresy out of the South, and hence closed the public forums to all antislavery doctrine. At the same time the fulminations of those abolitionists who allowed their opposition to slavery to lead them along the psychopathic trail to a hatred of slaveholders and who took special delight in foul invective and ribald abuse of everyone connected with the institution were cop-

ied into the Southern newspapers as a warning of the impending Northern plague. Perhaps it was inevitable that men who hated slavery should hate slaveholders. Perhaps it is just to lump the sinner with the sin. That is a matter of opinion. In any case it was not conducive to calm reflection or sympathetic understanding or a peaceable solution of the question. Year after year the Southerners went on enduring these charges of moral turpitude, with their holier-than-thou implications, nursing their wrath, and finding consolation in self-justification.

This catalogue of specific wrongs was also a part of the more general indictment of slavery as a sin. The antislavery movement was a powerful religious crusade, and religion played a far more important part in American life then than it does today. The Bible was presented as irrefutable proof that Jesus taught a doctrine of universal brotherhood; that man was created in the image of God; and that slavery reduced him to a piece of merchandise to be bought and sold in the market place. Said Theodore Weld, when the American Anti-Slavery Society was organized: "God has committed to every moral agent the privilege, the right and the responsibility of personal ownership. This is God's plan. Slavery annihilates it, and surrenders to avarice, passion and lust, all that makes life a blessing. It crushes the body, tramples into the dust the upward tendencies of the intellect, breaks the heart and kills the soul." Said the Central Executive Committee: "Every man who has put on the armor of Jesus Christ is under the paramount pledge to do all in his power for the salvation of the souls for which He died. How can you, my brother, do more than by *now* espousing the cause of those for whose souls there are *no men* to care." Slavery was denounced as a sin, "always, everywhere and only sin," *aside* from the evils of its administration. Abolitionists demanded that slaveholders be excluded from the pulpits of Northern churches and from the privileges of the sacraments, and those Southerners who finally championed the cause of secession lingered long on this aspect of the cause for action. Said the distinguished John S. Preston of South Carolina before the Virginia Convention: "This diversity at this moment is appearing not in forms of denominational polemics, but in shapes as bloody and terrible as religion has ever assumed since Christ came to earth. Its representative, the Church, has bared her arm for the conflict—her sword is already flashing in the glare of the torch of fanaticism—and the history of the world tells us that when that sword cleaves asunder, no human surgery can heal the wound. There is not one Christian slaveholder here, no matter how near he may be to his meek and lowly master, who does not feel in his heart that from the point of that sword is now dripping the last drop of sympathy which bound him to his brethren at the North. With demoniac rage they have set the Lamb of God between their seed and our seed."

In support of their charge that these violations of the standards of contemporary civilization were far more prevalent than Southerners were willing to admit, were inherent in slavery, and were indicative of the general moral tone of the institution, abolitionists presented a line of argument which was not easily contradicted. Slaves were property. They were bought and sold. The purchase price alone determined who might be a slaveholder. Society set no standards of intelligence, character, or

integrity for slaveholding. There were no public or private agencies charged with responsibility for the slave's welfare. Human nature being what it is or, better still, what it then was, what security was there for the individual slave against abuse of arbitrary power? Said Weld: "Arbitrary power is to the mind what alcohol is to the body; it intoxicates. It is perhaps the strongest human passion; and the more absolute the power, the stronger the desire for it; and the more it is desired, the more its exercise is enjoyed. . . . The fact that a person intensely desires power over others, *without restraint*, shows the absolute necessity of restraint." This condition was greatly aggravated by the fact that slaves were subject not only to the will of their owner, but to the authority of every white person with whom they came in contact off the owner's property, and to the slightest whim of the owner's family, even of children too immature to have disciplined themselves; and by the further fact that, in spite of abject servility and personal desire to suppress emotions, evidences of resentment must have been a common occurrence. "The idea of *property* having a will," said Weld, "and that too in opposition to the will of its *owner*, and counteracting it, is a stimulant of terrible power to the most relentless human passions." In support of his logic he brought together in *American Slavery As It Is* what he chose to call the "testimony of a thousand witnesses," the most devastating arraignment of slavery ever published. Hundreds of thousands of copies of the pamphlet were distributed, and its influence was incalculable. There was no effective reply to it, nor could there have been.

Not only did abolitionists examine slavery in the light of the Scriptures and of the moral standards prevailing in contemporary civilization; they also pronounced it contrary to the fundamental principles of the American way of life because it plundered the slaves of their inalienable rights as men: ownership of their own bodies; freedom of choice, as to use of time and to occupation; the rights of marriage, family life, and paternal authority; the right to worship according to conscience; the right to cultivate their minds, utilize their peculiar talents and influence their fellow men; the right to protect themselves, their homes, and their families against violence; the right to the protection of the law. These were things which, especially in those days of rugged individualism, made a powerful impression upon the average American.

The lack of legal protection for the slave constituted the greatest single indictment against the slaveholding states. The slave owner had no restraint but his own will over the type and amount of labor assigned to the slave. He might hire him out to other men; he might permit him to labor on his own account and claim his wages; he might inflict any kind or degree of punishment without fear of redress; he might assign absolute authority over the slave to any agent. He might sell the slave at will. The slave was both a chattel and real estate and liable to be sold in satisfaction of debts. He could not testify in court in any case involving a white man. If he raised his hand against a white man in any circumstances whatsoever, the penalty was death. He had no recourse against intolerable conditions but perilous flight. He could own no property, make no contracts, receive no education, claim no religious instruction. Whatever legislation had been passed with respect to slaves was purely for protection of property rights and the se-

curity of the institution. One may find, only rarely, feeble recognition by legislatures and courts of slaves as human beings. This was slavery's most vulnerable spot and was so considered by the abolitionists.

The practical application of the law, said the apologists for slavery, was far less rigorous than the provisions of the law, which was simply ignoring the point at issue. When they spoke of the slave codes as being unenforced except at rare intervals when mass hysteria followed attempted insurrections, a particularly brutal murder, or the apprehension of a suspected incendiary, they were speaking of laws passed for the protection of society, i.e. laws forbidding slaves to assemble without the presence of a white person; forbidding slaves to leave their owners' premises without a written permit; forbidding slaves to preach or masters to teach them to read; and requiring the regular patrol of all public highways. The important point is that that great body of law, both common and statute, and the courts, the instrument of its operation, to which men have looked since time immemorial for the administration of justice and for the protection of their most elementary human rights simply did not exist for three million slaves. Privileges they might have and no doubt did enjoy in generous measure from indulgent masters, but they had no more semblance of rights than the beasts of the field.

More difficult to evaluate with respect to its place in the Northern educational program was the abolition argument concerning the effect of slavery upon the two races and upon the South from the viewpoint of general culture and economy. This was in the nature of a rebuttal to the positive-good argument, the development of which preceded the abolition crusade of the thirties. The positive-good dogma embraced four theses: (1) that slave labor was essential to the development and continued prosperity of the southern country; (2) that the Negro race was inferior and destined by nature to a subordinate position; (3) that slavery had lifted a savage people from barbarism to Christian civilization; and (4) that the white race had not degenerated as a consequence, but, on the contrary, had developed a unique and high degree of culture. Ancillary to these there were, of course, a number of supporting theses. Divine sanction was invoked for the institution with the Bible as evidence. Historical precedent of the existence of slavery in every age was cited. Culture, it was said, could thrive only if the few enjoyed leisure from exploitation of the many, and Negro slavery threw wide the door of opportunity to all white men by substituting race exploitation for class exploitation. Southern bond slavery was compared to Northern wage slavery to prove that the Negro slave shared more abundantly in the necessaries of life than the Northern wage earner.

Much of the abolitionists' reply to the Southern claims of cultural superiority and the defense of slavery as a humane and civilizing institution is to be found in the general indictments of slavery as a sin and as incompatible with the standards of contemporary civilization. They did not hesitate, however, to meet the argument on specific points, twitting the slaveholders about their lack of a common school system, their resort to murder under the *code duello* for the satisfaction of every fancied wrong, their compulsory diversion of all mixed blood back into the Negro race to hide the shame of their immorality, and their propensity for gambling and hard drink-

ing. They ridiculed the idea that a system which made the happiness of a defenseless people "the sport of every whim, and the prey of every passion that may . . . infest the master's bosom" could possibly develop a profound sense of responsibility in the slaveholder, holding that the "daily practice of forcibly robbing others and habitually living on the plunder can not but beget in the mind the *habit* of regarding the interests and happiness of those whom it robs, as of no sort of consequence in comparison with its own." As for the slave, his very dependence impaired his manliness and independence of character, crushed his soul, and destroyed his ability to distinguish right from wrong. It cultivated immorality, placed a premium upon deception, and made lying and stealing acts of self-preservation.

The Bible argument waxed long and furiously, with perhaps a slight advantage to the abolitionists. Over the long view it appears to have been a rather fruitless discussion, without much influence one way or the other. Slavery's rôle in history was assessed as a liability rather than as a contribution to the glory and stability of Rome. It was condemned as an impediment to a balanced economy in the South, absorbing the capital necessary to industrial enterprise, denying the entrepreneur the public coöperation essential to the development of manufacturing, destroying the fertility of the soil through forced and incompetent labor, driving the non-slaveholder to the free states or ever farther back upon the margin of a bare subsistence level, turning the stream of foreign immigration elsewhere, and creating a contempt for manual labor on the part of the whites, the fruits of which were indolence on the one hand and arrogant snobbery on the other.

Finally, slavery was condemned as a menace to the peace and safety of the nation. Concentration of Negroes in the Black Belt entered into every phase of the slavery question. From the earliest days the champions of slavery had admitted the necessity of maintaining a proper ratio between the two races. The subject arose in connection with colonization. Southern pamphleteers conceded the desirability of diffusion as an aid to the alleviation of the system's harsher features. Fear of insurrection increased as the center of the slave population moved steadily toward the Southwest. It was advanced in defense of the prohibition against teaching slaves to read, permitting them to assemble without the presence of whites, etc. It played an important part in the discussion over the expansion of slave territory and in the Confederate Constitutional Convention with respect to the non-seceding states in 1861.

Abolitionists took particular delight, it would seem, in playing upon this fear of the South by exposing it as a national weakness, calling attention to the vulnerability of the southern coast to attack, chiding the South for dependence upon the great strength of the nation to protect from outside interference and from internal combustion an institution it insisted upon regarding as its own domestic concern, lashing out with bitter invective against the slavocracy for involving the whole nation in a war of conquest, and bringing all the pressure at their command against the state department's representations to Great Britain in the *Creole* and other cases.

The particular emphasis placed upon each of these several indictments depended upon the time, the occasion, and the person discussing the subject. It is essential to remember that the antislav-

ery movement was almost completely unorganized until the founding of the American Anti-Slavery Society in December, 1833. There were the New York City Manumission Society, organized by John Jay and Alexander Hamilton in 1785; the Pennsylvania Abolition Society, organized by Benjamin Franklin in 1789; and scattered local societies in North Carolina, Tennessee, and southern Ohio; but the organized movement for the entire abolition of slavery in the United States began in the early thirties. From 1833 to 1840 it was under the direction of a powerful executive committee of the American Anti-Slavery Society, located in New York City. After 1839 there were two national organizations: the American Anti-Slavery Society, under the control of William Lloyd Garrison at Boston, and the American and Foreign Anti-Slavery Society, under the control of Lewis Tappan in New York City. During the first period work was carried on largely through local and traveling agents and was predominantly religious, with churches the forums, the sin of slavery the theme, and the organization of state and local auxiliary societies and the founding of antislavery newspapers an important function of the agents. After 1840 neither of the national organizations exercised much influence or control over the movement; but, so far as they did, the American and Foreign Anti-Slavery Society was the functional continuation of the original American Anti-Slavery Society, distinctly religious and friendly to the churches and promoting the old policy of seeking the abolition of slavery by moral suasion. The real work of maintaining agencies and newspapers and depositories for antislavery literature, however, was carried on by the powerful state societies. The function of giving direction to the movement and defining its objectives was now under the control of a small group of politically minded abolitionists, and state societies shortly became almost identical with state antislavery political parties. The American Anti-Slavery Society under Garrison at Boston— the old society name without the substance—was distinctly antichurch, antipolitical, and strongly flavored with peace, no-human-government, and woman's rights. . . .

Men like Theodore Weld and Julius LeMoyne were not convinced that political action was "*essential* as a means to the great end in view." They looked upon it as only another distracting issue such as woman's rights, no-human-government, and peace—collateral questions which would "divide, distract, embarrass and alienate the abolition body, and . . . divert their attention and efforts from the first and grand object." This was particularly true, said LeMoyne, because, "except for the *single object* of our association, no body of men who are associated, are composed of such various and almost incongruous materials—men of all religions and no religion—of all politics and shades of policy—of all habits of thought and prejudices of education and locality—which our country furnishes example." To this reason for opposition they added the fear of revealing the paucity of their numbers, the impropriety of undertaking to promote a religious enterprise by means of an essentially different character, and the possibility of the movement falling under the control of politicians and vote-getting expediency supplanting principle to the end of an abandonment of high antislavery ground. . . .

Most antislavery men, among the rank and file, were opposed to independent political action in the beginning, largely of course, because they were good Whigs or good Democrats. Political creeds were an inheritance and a habit, soul-deadening and death-defying. However much men might deprecate the proslavery bent of their party leaders and party platforms, or be willing to annoy them with embarrassing questions relative to slavery, they were not willing to take any action which might lead to the dissolution of their party or to withhold a vote which might enable the opposition to win. Slavery was an important issue, one capable of sorely disturbing the conscience and freighted with dire consequences to the national security, but so were other things—banking, for instance, or the tariff, or internal improvement, or the disposition of the public lands—and men were not willing to forego registering a vote on such questions, even though they appreciated the importance of a powerful protest vote against slavery domination of the old line parties.

To all such staunch party men Birney wrote: "The security of life—of liberty —of civil and religious privileges—of the rights of conscience—of the right to use our own faculties for the promotion of our own happiness—of free locomotion, —all these, together with the defence of the barriers and outposts thrown around them by the laws, constitute the highest concerns of the government. These, for the last six years, we have seen invaded one after another—the administration aiding in the onset—till the *feeling of security* for any of them has well nigh expired. A censorship of the mail is usurped by the deputy postmasters throughout more than half of the country, and approved by the administration under which it takes place. The pillage of the Post Office is perpetrated in one of our principal cities, and its contents made a bonfire of in the public square;

—no one is brought in question for the outrage. Free speech and debate on the most important subject that now agitates the country, is rendered impossible in our national legislature; the *right* of the people to petition Congress for a redress of grievances is formally abolished by their own servants! And shall we sit down and dispute about the currency, about a subtreasury or no-sub-treasury, a bank or no-bank, while such outrages on constitutional and essential *rights* are enacting before our eyes?"

Many of those who first supported independent political action were convinced of its efficacy as a method of rendering slavery odious and of forcing one or the other of the old parties to adopt a firmer stand against slavery. So far as Myron Holley, James G. Birney, Alvan Stewart, Joshua Leavitt, William Goodell, and others were concerned, however, it represented a settled conviction that the attempt to maintain a harmonious union between sections with such diametrically opposite principles was impossible, and that the time had come for those who believed in the republican principles and habits of the Northern states to make a militant stroke for control of the federal government and thereby gain complete ascendency over the slave power. It was the first step in the formation of two great sectional parties which were to contend for control of the government in 1860, and men knew it to be so. Said Weld: "Nothing short of miracles, constant miracles, and such as the world has never seen can keep at bay the two great antagonist forces. . . . They must drive against each other, till *one* of them goes to the bottom. *Events,* the master of men, have for years been silently but without a moment's pause, settling the basis of two great parties, the nucleus of one slavery, of the other freedom. . . ."

II. THE CONTEMPORARY DEBATE OVER ABOLITIONIST METHODS

William Lloyd Garrison: TO THE PUBLIC

The following statement of aims by William Lloyd Garrison (1805– 1879) in the first issue of his journal, The Liberator, *is one of the most quoted documents in American history. Small though its circulation was, the launching of this journal on its thirty-five-year career symbolized and in a measure caused the emergence of immediate abolitionism as a powerful reform impulse. Besides the famous Garrisonian rhetoric, this editorial reveals how early abolitionists were forced to debate the question of means.*

IN THE month of August, I issued proposals for publishing "THE LIBERATOR" in Washington City; but the enterprise, though hailed in different sections of the country, was palsied by public indifference. Since that time, the removal of the *Genius of Universal Emancipation* to the Seat of Government has rendered less imperious the establishment of a similar periodical in that quarter.

During my recent tour for the purpose of exciting the minds of the people by a series of discourses on the subject of slavery, every place that I visited gave fresh evidence of the fact, that a greater revolution in public sentiment was to be effected in the free States— *and particularly in New-England*—than at the South. I found contempt more bitter, opposition more active, detraction more relentless, prejudice more stubborn, and apathy more frozen, than among slave-owners themselves. Of course, there were individual exceptions to the contrary. This state of things

afflicted, but did not dishearten me. I determined, at every hazard, to lift up the standard of emancipation in the eyes of the nation, *within sight of Bunker Hill and in the birthplace of liberty.* That standard is now unfurled; and long may it float, unhurt by the spoliations of time or the missiles of a desperate foe— yea, till very chain be broken, and every bondman set free! Let Southern oppressors tremble—let their secret abettors tremble—let their Northern apologists tremble—let all the enemies of the persecuted blacks tremble.

I deem the publication of my original Prospectus unnecessary, as it has obtained a wide circulation. The principles therein inculcated will be steadily pursued in this paper, excepting that I shall not array myself as the political partisan of any man. In defending the great cause of human rights, I wish to derive the assistance of all religions and of all parties.

Assenting to the "self-evident truth" maintained in the American Declara-

From Wendell Phillips Garrison and Francis Jackson Garrison, *William Lloyd Garrison, 1805– 1879: The Story of His Life Told by His Children* (New York: The Century Company, 1885), Vol. I, pp. 224–26.

tion of Independence, "that all men are created equal, and endowed by their Creator with certain inalienable rights— among which are life, liberty and the pursuit of happiness," I shall strenuously contend for the immediate enfranchisement of our slave population. In Park-Street Church, on the Fourth of July, 1829, in an address on slavery, I unreflectingly assented to the popular but pernicious doctrine of *gradual* abolition. I seize this opportunity to make a full and unequivocal recantation, and thus publicly to ask pardon of my God, of my country, and of my brethren the poor slaves, for having uttered a sentiment so full of timidity, injustice, and absurdity. A similar recantation, from my pen, was published in the *Genius of Universal Emancipation* at Baltimore, in September, 1829. My conscience is now satisfied.

I am aware that many object to the severity of my language; but is there not cause for severity? I *will be* as harsh as truth, and as uncompromising as justice. On this subject, I do not wish to think, or speak, or write, with moderation. No! no! Tell a man whose house in on fire to give a moderate alarm; tell him to moderately rescue his wife from the hands of the ravisher; tell the mother to gradually extricate her babe from the fire into which it has fallen;—but urge me not to use moderation in a cause like the present. I am in earnest—I will not equivocate—I will not excuse—I will not retreat a single inch—AND I WILL BE HEARD. The apathy of the people is enough to make every statue leap from its pedestal, and to hasten the resurrection of the dead.

It is pretended, that I am retarding the cause of emancipation by the coarseness of my invective and the precipitancy of my measures. *The charge is not true.* On this question my influence,— humble as it is,—is felt at this moment to a considerable extent, and shall be felt in coming years—not perniciously, but beneficially—not as a curse, but as a blessing; and posterity will bear testimony that I was right. I desire to thank God, that he enables me to disregard "the fear of man which bringeth a snare," and to speak his truth in its simplicity and power. And here I close with this fresh dedication:

"Oppression! I have seen thee, face to face,
  And met thy cruel eye and cloudy brow;
  But thy soul-withering glance I fear not
    now—
  For dread to prouder feelings doth give
    place
  Of deep abhorrence! Scorning the disgrace
  Of slavish knees that at thy footstool bow,
  I also kneel—but with far other vow
  Do hail thee and thy herd of hirelings
    base:—
  I swear, while life-blood warms my throbbing veins,
  Still to oppose and thwart, with heart and
    hand,
  Thy brutalising sway—till Afric's chains
  Are burst, and Freedom rules the rescued
    land,—
  Trampling Oppression and his iron rod:
  Such is the vow I take—SO HELP ME GOD!"

WILLIAM LLOYD GARRISON.
BOSTON, January 1, 1831.

Anonymous: THE SOUTH VINDICATED FROM THE TREASON AND FANATICISM OF THE NORTHERN ABOLITIONISTS

In an introductory statement that gives a clue to his regional background, the unknown author of the following passages writes, "We do not, at the North, claim a right so to discuss this subject as to disturb or agitate the South; but when reckless men have sent forth, for the worst purposes, hosts of falsehoods, it is our right and duty to step aside and crush the misbegotten and dangerous brood." His quotations from antislavery publications and his references to specific incidents reveal close attention to abolitionist activities. The colonizationists he judges as showing "justice, purity, and patriotism," though he considers their program ineffective. The book includes an elaborate defense of slavery, but the parts here reproduced are those dealing with the goals and methods of immediate abolitionists.

WE WILL now consider the scheme of emancipation—a scheme which, but a few years since, found our country united, tranquil and happy, and which, in that brief period, has planted in her bosom distrust, jealousy, rage and terror—which has endangered the industry of the North, the security of life in the South, and has shaken to its very centre the Government of our common country.

The object of those who have espoused the cause of the slave is averred to be emancipation. They pronounce his bondage a sin against heaven, and claim the freedom of every negro in the country—young and old, male and female, ignorant and educated. Universal and sweeping emancipation is the object of their efforts; and they express their determination never to remit their exertions until the two millions of slaves in the South are released from all restraint.

This emancipation is claimed *immediately.* They will not submit to any gradual measures for the attainment of their wishes. The word is to be spoken by these necromancers in philanthropy, and the chains of the 2,250,000 slaves are to be shivered, as by one blow. The negro is to be instantaneously released, and turned forth, without the intelligence to direct his conduct, the habits of self restraint to withhold him from the brutal gratification of animal passions, or even the means of saving himself from starvation. When asked, what will be the consequences of so mad and precipitate a movement, they inform us that consequences do not enter into their calculations—slavery is a sin, of which the slave-holder should repent, not gradually, but at once—the consequences of his repentance rest with Providence. That we may not misrepresent their views on this important point, we give the following extract from one of the publications of the American Anti-Slavery Society. . . .

"Gradual Abolition, an indefinite term, but which is understood to imply the

From *The South Vindicated from the Treason and Fanaticism of the Northern Abolitionists* (Philadelphia: H. Manly, 1836), pp. 150–54, 157–61, 163, 168–70, 285–87.

draining away drop by drop of the great ocean of wrongs,—plucking off at long intervals some straggling branches of the moral Upas—holding out to unborn generations the shadow of a hope which the present may never feel,—gradually ceasing to do evil; gradually refraining from robbery, lust and murder;—in brief, obeying a short-sighted and criminal policy rather than the commands of God."

The immediate emancipation, thus claimed for the blacks, is required to be unconditional. They admit no restraint upon the negro. He is to be turned loose at once. No barrier, no bond, no check, —nothing to guard the negroes from their own improvidence and passions, nothing to protect the master or his wife and daughters from the savage passions, the lust, revenge and cruelty of the brutal and unchained slave. . . .

The emancipation, thus urged, is expected to be attained without compensation to the master. It is of no consequence that not merely individuals, but States, would be thus beggared; that those gentle beings, who have been nurtured with all the solicitude of affection, and treated with the homage of Southern chivalry—that those fair creatures, whose guardians

> Would not permit the winds of Heaven
> Visit their cheeks too roughly,—

thus fostered, are, by Northern philanthropists to be plunged into the most sordid poverty, and, as they are inferior to the blacks in capacity for toil, to be degraded beneath those who have heretofore ministered to their wants. The slave-holder, says the abolitionist, is a "robber," a "felon," a "man-stealer," &c., and has no right to expect that, when deprived of his victim, he will be paid for his past crimes in the shape of compensation or ransom! The fanatics are mar-

vellously philanthropic: they would beggar and ruin the citizens of the South to realize their childish abstractions; but they [had] not yet attained that point of delusion which would prompt them to bear a share of the burthen. Men can afford to be charitable, who give away the property of others; and none urge self-denial so ardently as those who are not called upon to participate in the sacrifice. The abolitionists, in advocating emancipation without compensation, do not forget, but do not regard, the fact, that the slaves have fallen into the hands of their present owners as *property*, that the laws of the Southern States, the laws of the General Government, and even the laws of the Northern States, regard them and respect them, *as property*. These facts are wholly immaterial to the abolitionists. The obligation of justice, the sanction of the laws, the rights of humanity, are subjects of equal indifference to those who are prepared to stride over the graves of millions of their brethren, over the ruins of their Government and country, to the consummation of their visionary and perilous schemes. . . .

But a few years have elapsed since the commencement of the abolition movement. It originated in a few heated and disturbed minds, and was urged in the face of every obstacle. Wm. Lloyd Garrison, Lundy, and some others, who conceived themselves the chosen instruments of accomplishing abolition, proclaimed their peculiar doctrines with an ardour, which, if it did not excite respect, at least attracted attention. Garrison, the most talented and rabid of the corps, soon became notorious. In the fury of his zeal he did not scruple to borrow the aid of fiction; and, at times, indulged his talent for invective, at the expense of truth, and of the character of respectable citizens. The difficulties into which this unfortunate propensity plunged him, only excited his ardour anew. The strict confinement and low diet to which the irreverend administrators of the law consigned him, did not allay the violence of his zeal. He regarded his misfortune as a partial martyrdom. It certainly had one advantage—it lifted him to an elevation which, like that of the pillory, rendered him the observed of all observers. He renewed his denunciations with spirit. He raved, and the world laughed; but in the end he proved that, so ricketty and unstable a thing is the world, even the efforts of a madman can disturb it. He gained disciples—what fanatic ever raved without converts?—and soon became an object of attention to the crack-brained enthusiasts and antiquated ladies of the whole land. The Colonization Society had, by agitating the subject, prepared the country for the coming of this second Peter the Hermit; and the crusade preached by him against the institutions of the South, found supporters and advocates. At length, he enlisted a sufficient force in behalf of abolition, to enable him to visit England, and crave foreign influence against the laws and lives of his fellow countrymen. England was herself reeling under the potions of quacks and enthusiasts, and lent a willing ear to the crazed abstractions, wild appeals, and exaggerated statements, of Garrison. He found himself in his element. He preached against his country to applauding multitudes; he denounced Washington as a robber, because a slave-holder; characterized the American Constitution as a guilty and blood-stained instrument, because it recognized the domestic laws of the South; and, in short, indulged, to his heart's content, in foul and frothy invective against all that is dear and sacred to Americans. Having sufficiently

blackened his country abroad, he returned to renew his treasonable efforts at home. He was received by the fanatics with rapture; and the work was resumed with fresh ardour. The efforts of these conspirators, at their midnight meetings, where the bubbling cauldron of abolition was filled with its pestiential materials, and the fire beneath kindled by the breath of the fanatics, has often reminded us of the witch scene in Macbeth. Their chorus is peculiarly in character for the amalgamationists.

> "Black spirits and white,
> Red spirits and gray,
> Mingle, mingle, mingle,
> You that mingle may."

It requires no excited imagination to conceive them gathered in their secret councils, where, at first, a few half-crazed enthusiasts, with a bevy of female fanatics, met to hatch and prepare this precious scheme. In such a conclave, assembled for such a purpose, the incantation of the scene referred to, would have been wholly appropriate.

> "For a charm of powerful trouble,
> Like a hell-broth, boil and bubble.
> Double, double, toil and trouble,
> Fire burn and cauldron bubble!"

In these scenes we may suppose that Garrison, gloomy, wild, and malignant, was the ruling spirit. His religious madness, his vehement cant and violence of spirit naturally gained for him the mastery in their councils. Whatever may be the character of his coadjutors, Garrison has, in his whole career, betrayed the worst purposes allied to the worst passions. His writings have been blackened with the vilest slanders, and the most vindictive abuse. Indeed, so vehement, rancorous and fiend-like have been his exhibitions of passion against his opponents, that most persons have considered, and do still consider, him insane. It is a probable and certainly a charitable supposition; for if he is to be considered as strictly accountable for his ravings, he must be held in general execration. The following extract from his writings is a specimen of his style, and certainly affords no evidence of the soundness of either his head or his heart. He addresses the slave-holders. The reader will be reminded of the celebrated sermon of Maw-worm.

"Ye crafty calculators! Ye hard-hearted incorrigible sinners! Ye greedy and relentless robbers! Ye contemners of justice and mercy! Ye trembling, pitiful, pale-faced usurpers! My soul spurns you with unspeakable disgust!"

The style of Garrison is turgid, but often effective. His compositions appear intended to operate principally upon the ignorant blacks; and are filled with declamation, denunciation and cant. In abusing his opponents, he exhibits a frantic and frontless disregard of the decencies of the press. In advocating his doctrines, he pauses at no difficulty. If good men sanction slavery—they are robbers; if the Constitution maintains it —it must be crushed; if the Union is an obstacle—it must be overthrown. He never writes without raving; he even reasons like a bedlamite; and in his paper, which has great influence over the blacks, he has done much to excite a spirit of insubordination and violence.

Until recently, these outrages were allowed to pass unpunished; but the time has at length arrived when a wronged and insulted people will no longer permit these madmen to tamper with the peace and welfare of our country. The citizens of Boston recently took possession of the person of Garrison, with a view to summary punishment, and were only deterred by compassion, from bestowing on him the honorary ointment and robe which has, time immemorial, been decreed in the East to traitors. He was, however, committed to prison as a protection from the just indignation of the people, and in the morning escaped from the city in disguise.

Perhaps, after Garrison, the noted Arthur Tappan solicits the next place in the roll of the abolitionists. He is a well known and wealthy merchant of New York, who has become affluent by the patronage of those whom he is so eager to expose to the horrors of a servile insurrection. He is generally described as an amiable, weak, well-meaning man, whose limited portion of intellect has been turned topsy-turvy by religious excitement. He has not sufficient mind to originate, or resist, any religious delusion. He is made the dupe of every fanatic or imposter, who thunders religious denunciations in his ears. New York appears to have been for some years afflicted with a prevailing tendency to fanaticism. Not a fanatic so stupid, but in New York he could find admirers; not an impostor so degraded, but in New York he could enlist followers. . . .

It may be doubted, notwithstanding Mr. Tappan's fanaticism, whether his piety would have pressed him into so conspicuous a station among the abolitionists, had not another passion pleaded in its favour. Weak men are generally vain. Incapable of great or useful ambition; they cherish a pruriency for praise, or an anxiety to escape from their natural insignificance, by notoriety of any kind. Even abuse is grateful to them, for it is an acknowledgment of their importance; the praise and censure incurred by Mr. Tappan are acceptable incense to him, and are purchased cheaply by his large contributions to the abolitionists. He finds himself rendered, by his connection with them, "a marvellous proper man," and clings with delight to a cause which has ministered so successfully to the little vanity of a feeble and contracted mind. . . .

We will not enter further into an account of the leaders of the abolition conspiracy. It is unnecessary to describe the *Reverend* Dr. Beman of Troy, one of the most noisy and violent of the canting supporters of abolition, who *first sold out his slaves,* and then denounced those "who sell the image of Jesus." It is equally unnecessary to refer particularly to the Rev. Dr. Cox, who pronounced Jesus Christ a coloured man; or to Mr. Thorne who said—"The slave States are *Sodoms* and almost every village family *a brothel.*" Or to the Reverend Mr. May, who preaches that the Constitution *ought to be violated* if counter to what *he* considers the will of Heaven; or to scores of others, whose violence and extravagance have excited, in every reasonable citizen, sentiments of alarm and disgust. . . .

It is painful to know, that there are men, who regard the prospect of disunion, without emotion, and who are determined to urge their insane projects, indifferent what barriers are broken down, what altars overthrown, what sacrifices made. To them the recollection of our common war of independence, where the North stood breast to breast with the South, when they poured out their blood, like water, beneath the same proud flag, and in the same holy cause—appeals in vain. The glory of the past, the hopes of the future, are nothing to them. They are willing to see the land of Washington—the glory and pride of the earth—shattered, overthrown and trampled in the dust—her past glories blotted out—her future hopes forever blasted. To such men nothing is sacred.

They will follow their phantom—rending asunder the holiest ties, and bringing shame and ruin upon all that should be dear to them.

Yet they ask credit for their motives! A word on this point. It is generally unsafe to judge men's motives by any other test than their actions. If a man places a torch to a magazine, the explosion of which must destroy a city, and tells you, when his arm is arrested, that his motives are good—you would decide, that the man was either a dangerous madman, who should be chained, or a guilty miscreant, who would perpetrate the worst crimes under the holiest pretences. Men never avow evil motives. The vilest felon has recourse to this paltry defence; and the act which cannot borrow so poor a gloss, so thin and common a veil, must be base and black indeed. Hell itself, the proverb tells us, is paved with good intentions. Until we find some more satisfactory explanation of the course of the abolitionists, we cannot see them busy in their work of agitation—

"While at their feet,
Leashed in like hounds, famine, and sword, and fire,
Crouch for employment,"—

we cannot see them coolly promoting the horrors of civil discord, and hold them guiltless on the score of pure intentions. Were there room for error, they might plead the soundness of their motives. But how can they be deceived? They have already sown the wind and reaped the whirlwind. Riots and violence in the North, popular indignation and servile insurrection at the South—are the first and only fruits of their efforts. Can they point us to any good they have accomplished, or can reasonably hope to accomplish? They cannot. They shut their eyes to the manifold and fearful consequences of their madness, exclaim, "we are doing our duty," and rush on in their headlong career. And they will continue to rush on until arrested by legislative interference; until they dash themselves to pieces against the rock of our Union; or until they have toppled that Union into the dust, and filled this happy country with the din, and guilt, and terrors of fratricidal and fraternal warfare.

Charles Hodge: THE EFFECTS OF ABOLITIONISM

Although most denominations handled the slavery question gingerly during the 1830s, the Lutherans, Dutch Reformed, and Old School Presbyterians were notably unwilling to brand all slave-holders sinners. A leading theological spokesman for these orthodox Calvinists was Charles Hodge (1797–1878), professor in Princeton Theological Seminary. Most of his writing on this subject sought to prove that the Bible did not condemn all slave-holding. In the following passage, however, Hodge deals with the practicality of proposals for immediate abolition. The article first appeared in the Biblical Repertory and Theological Review *of April, 1836, as a review of William Ellery Channing's* Slavery.

EVERY one must be sensible that a very great change has, within a few years, been produced in the feelings, if not in the opinions of the public, in relation to slavery. It is not long since the acknowledgment was frequent at the South and universal at the North, that it was a great evil. It was spoken of in the slaveholding States, as a sad inheritance fixed upon them by the cupidity of the mother-country in spite of their repeated remonstrances. The known sentiments of Jefferson were reiterated again and again in every part of his native State; and some of the strongest denunciations of this evil, and some of the most ardent aspirations for deliverance from it ever uttered in the country, were pronounced, but a few years since, in the legislature of Virginia. A proposition to call a convention, with the purpose of so amending the constitution of the State as to admit of the general emancipation of the slaves, is said to have failed in the legislature of Kentucky by a single vote.[1] The sentiments of the northern States had long since been clearly expressed by the abolition of slavery within their limits. That the same opinions and the same feelings continued to prevail among them, may be inferred, not only from the absence of all evidence to the contrary, but from various decisive indications of a positive

[1] It is probable that many reasons combined to make a convention desirable to those who voted for it. But to get rid of slavery was said to be one of the most prominent.

From Charles Hodge, *Essays and Reviews* (New York: Robert and Carter Brothers, 1857), pp. 473–77.

character. In the year 1828 a resolution was passed by an almost unanimous vote in the legislature of Pennsylvania, instructing their Senators in Congress to endeavor to procure the passage of a law abolishing slavery in the District of Columbia. In 1829 a similar resolution was adopted by the assembly of New York. In 1828 a petition to this effect was presented to Congress, signed by one thousand inhabitants of the District itself; and the House of Representatives instructed the proper committee, in 1829, to inquire into the expediency of the measure. How altered is the present state of the country! Instead of lamentations and acknowledgments, we hear from the South the strongest language of justification. And at the North, opposition to the proceedings of the anti-slavery societies seems to be rapidly producing a public feeling in favor of slavery itself. The freedom of discussion, the liberty of the press, and the right of assembling for consultation, have in some cases been assailed, and in others trampled under foot by popular violence. What has produced this lamentable change? No doubt, many circumstances have combined in its production. We think, however, that all impartial observers must acknowledge, that by far the most prominent cause is the conduct of the abolitionists. They, indeed, naturally resist this imputation and endeavor to show its injustice by appealing to the fact that their opinions of slavery have been entertained and expressed by many of the best men of former days. This appeal, however, is by no means satisfactory. The evil in question has been produced by no mere expression of opinion. Had the abolitionists confined themselves to their professed object, and endeavored to effect their purpose by arguments addressed to the un-

derstandings and consciences of their fellow-citizens, no man could have had any reason to complain. Under ordinary circumstances, such arguments as those presented on this subject in Dr. Wayland's Elements of Moral Science, and in Dr. Channing's recent publication, would have been received with respect and kindness in every part of the country. We make this assertion, because the same sentiments, more offensively, and less ably urged, have heretofore been thus received.

It is not by argument that the abolitionists have produced the present unhappy excitement. Argument has not been the characteristic of their publications. Denunciations of slaveholding, as man-stealing, robbery, piracy, and worse than murder; consequent vituperation of slaveholders as knowingly guilty of the worst of crimes; passionate appeals to the feelings of the inhabitants of the northern States; gross exaggeration of the moral and physical condition of the slaves, have formed the staple of their addresses to the public. We do not mean to say that there has been no calm and Christian discussion on the subject. We mean merely to state what has, to the best of our knowledge, been the predominant character of the anti-slavery publications. There is one circumstance which renders the error and guilt of this course of conduct chargeable, in a great measure, on the abolitionists as a body, and even upon those of their number who have pursued a different course. We refer to the fact that they have upheld the most extreme publications, and made common cause with the most reckless declaimers. The wildest ravings of the *Liberator* have been constantly lauded; agents have been commissioned whose great distinction was a talent for eloquent vituperation; coincidence of opinion as to the single point of immediate emancipation has been sufficient to unite men of the most discordant character. There is in this conduct such a strange want of adaptation of the means to the end which they profess to have in view, as to stagger the faith of most persons in the sincerity of their professions, who do not consider the extremes to which even good men may be carried, when they allow one subject to take exclusive possession of their minds. We do not doubt their sincerity; but we marvel at their delusion. They seem to have been led by the mere impulse of feeling, and a blind imitation of their predecessors in England, to a course of measures, which, though rational under one set of circumstances, is the height of infatuation under another. The English abolitionists addressed themselves to a community, which, though it owned no slaves, had the power to abolish slavery, and was therefore responsible for its continuance. Their object was to rouse that community to immediate action. For this purpose they addressed themselves to the feelings of the people; they portrayed in the strongest colors the misery of the slaves; they dilated on the gratuitous crime of which England was guilty in perpetuating slavery, and did all they could to excite the passions of the public. This was the very course most likely to succeed, and it did succeed. Suppose, however, that the British parliament had no power over the subject; that it rested entirely with the colonial assemblies to decide whether slavery should be abolished or not. Does any man believe the abolitionists would have gained their object? Did they, in fact, make converts of the planters? Did they even pretend that such was their design? Every one knows that their conduct produced a state of almost frantic excitement in the West India Islands; that so far from the public feeling in England producing a moral impression upon the planters favorable to the condition of the slaves, its effect was directly the reverse. It excited them to drive away the missionaries, to tear down the chapels, to manifest a determination to rivet still more firmly the chains on their helpless captives, and to resist to the utmost all attempts for their emancipation or even improvement. All this was natural, though it was all, under the circumstances, of no avail, except to rouse the spirit of the mother-country, and to endanger the result of the experiment of emancipation, by exasperating the feelings of the slaves. Precisely similar has been the result of the efforts of the American abolitionists as it regards the slaveholders of America. They have produced a state of alarming exasperation at the South, injurious to the slave and dangerous to the country, while they have failed to enlist the feelings of the North. This failure has resulted, not so much from diversity of opinion on the abstract question of slavery, or from want of sympathy among nothern men in the cause of human rights, as from the fact that the common sense of the public has been shocked by the incongruity and folly of hoping to effect the abolition of slavery in one country by addressing the people of another. We do not expect to abolish despotism in Russia, by getting up indignation meetings in New York. Yet, for all the purposes of legislation on this subject, Russia is not more a foreign country to us than South Carolina. The idea of inducing the southern slaveholder to emancipate his slaves by denunciation, is about as rational as to expect the sovereigns of Europe to grant free institutions, by calling them tyrants and robbers. Could we send our denunciations of despotism among the subjects of those monarchs, and rouse the people to a sense of their wrongs and a determination to redress them, there would be some prospect of success. But our northern abolitionists disclaim, with great earnestness, all intention of allowing their appeals to reach the ears of the slaves. It is, therefore, not to be wondered at, that the course pursued by the anti-slavery societies, should produce exasperation at the South, without conciliating sympathy at the North. The impolicy of their conduct is so obvious, that men who agree with them as to all their leading principles, not only stand aloof from their measures, but unhesitatingly condemn their conduct. . . .

Angelina Grimké: LETTERS TO CATHERINE E. BEECHER

Born into an aristocratic slave-holding family in Charleston, South Carolina, Angelina Grimké (1805–1879) and her sister Sarah grew dissatisfied with the practice of slavery and the formalism of the Episcopal church. They moved north, became Quakers, and in time obtained their share of the family slaves and freed them. Angelina in 1836 published an antislavery pamphlet, Appeal to the Christian Women of the South, *and was promptly denounced in her native city. At a time when such public activity by women was considered immodest, even indecent, the sisters gave lectures on the need for abolition. The following open letters answered criticisms published by Catherine Beecher, daughter of Lyman Beecher, leading New School Presbyterian minister and president of Lane Seminary, and sister of the not-yet-famous Harriet Beecher Stowe. Miss Beecher's objections to Angelina's abolitionist activities are clear from the answering arguments. In 1838 Angelina married the man who had abolitionized Lane Seminary, Theodore Weld.*

LETTER I. FUNDAMENTAL PRINCIPLE
OF ABOLITIONISTS

Brookline, Mass. 6 month, 12th, 1837.

My Dear Friend: Thy book has appeared just at a time, when, from the nature of my engagements, it will be impossible for me to give it that attention which so weighty a subject demands. Incessantly occupied in prosecuting a mission, the responsibilities of which task all my powers, I can reply to it only by desultory letters, thrown from my pen as I travel from place to place. I prefer this mode to that of taking as long a time to answer it, as thou didst to determine upon the best method by which to counteract the effect of my testimony at the north—which, as the preface of thy book informs me, was thy main design.

Thou thinkest I have not been "suf-

From Angelina E. Grimké, *Letters to Catherine E. Beecher, in Reply to an Essay on Slavery and Abolitionism, Addressed to A. E. Grimké* (Boston: Isaac Knapp, 1838), pp. 3–4, 6–13, 29–32, 34, 51–57, 94–99.

ficiently informed in regard to the feelings and opinions of Christian females at the North" on the subject of slavery; for that in fact they hold the same *principles* with Abolitionists, although they condemn their measures. Wilt thou permit me to receive their principles from thy pen? Thus instructed, however misinformed I may heretofore have been, I can hardly fail of attaining to accurate knowledge. Let us examine them, to see how far they correspond with the principles held by Abolitionists.

The great fundamental principle of Abolitionists is, that man cannot rightfully hold his fellow man as property. Therefore, we affirm, that *every slaveholder is a man-stealer*. We do so, for the following reasons: to steal a man is to rob him of himself. It matters not whether this be done in Guinea, or Carolina; a man is a *man*, and *as* a man he has *inalienable* rights, among which is the right to personal *liberty*. Now if every man has an *inalienable* right to personal liberty, it follows, that he cannot rightfully be reduced to slavery. But I find in these United States, 2,250,000 men, women and children, robbed of that to which they have an *inalienable* right. How comes this to pass? Where millions are plundered, are there no *plunderers?* If, then, the slaves have been robbed of their liberty, *who* has robbed them? Not the man who stole their forefathers from Africa, but he who now holds them in bondage; no matter *how* they came into his possession, whether he inherited them, or bought them, or seized them at their birth on his own plantation. The only difference I can see between the original man-stealer, who caught the African in his native country, and the American slaveholder, is, that the former committed *one* act of robbery, while the

other perpetrates the same crime *continually*.

. . . These are Abolition sentiments on the subject of slaveholding; and although our principles are universally held by our opposers at the North, yet I am told on the 44th page of thy book, that "the word man-stealer has one peculiar signification, and is no more synonymous with slaveholder than it is with sheep-stealer." I must acknowledge, thou has only confirmed my opinion of the difference which I had believed to exist between Abolitionists and their opponents. As well might Saul have declared, that he held similar views with Stephen, when he stood by and kept the raiment of those who slew him.

I know that a broad line of distinction is drawn between our principles and our measures, by those who are anxious to "avoid the appearance of evil"— very desirous of retaining the fair character of enemies to slavery. Now, our *measures* are simply the carrying out of our *principles;* and we find, that just in proportion as individuals embrace our principles, in spirit and in truth, they cease to cavil at our measures. Gerrit Smith is a striking illustration of this. Who cavilled more at Anti-Slavery *measures,* and who more ready now to acknowledge his former blindness? Real Abolitionists know full well, that the slave never has been, and never can be, a whit the better for mere abstractions, floating in the *head* of any man; and they also know, that *principles, fixed in the heart,* are things of another sort. The former have never done any good in the world, because they possess no vitality, and therefore cannot bring forth *the fruits* of holy, untiring effort; but the latter live in the lives of their possessors, and breathe in their words. And I am free to express my belief, that *all* who really and heartily approve our *principles*, will also approve our *measures;* and that, too, just as certainly as a good tree will bring forth good fruit.

But there is another peculiarity in the views of Abolitionists. We hold that the North is guilty of the crime of slave-holding—we assert that it is a *national* sin: on the contrary, in thy book, I find the following acknowledgement:—"*Most* persons in the non-slaveholding States, have considered the matter of southern slavery as one in which they were no more called to interfere, than in the abolition of the press-gang system in England, or the tithe-system in Ireland." Now I cannot see how the same principles can produce such entirely different opinions. "Can a good tree bring forth corrupt fruit?" This I deny, and cannot admit what thou art anxious to prove, viz. that "Public opinion may have been *wrong* on this point, and yet *right* on all those great *principles* of rectitude and justice relating to slavery." If Abolition principles are generally adopted at the North, how comes it to pass, that there is no abolition action here, except what is put forth by a few despised fanatics, as they are called? Is there any living faith without works? Can the sap circulate vigorously, and yet neither blossoms put forth nor fruit appear?

Again, I am told on the 7th page, that all Northern Christians believe it is a sin to hold a man in slavery for "*mere purposes of gain;*" as if this was the *whole* abolition principle on this subject. I can assure thee that Abolitionists do not stop here. Our principle is, that *no circumstances can ever justify* a man in holding his fellow man as *property;* it matters not what *motive* he may give

for such a monstrous violation of the laws of God. The claim to him as *property* is an annihilation of his right to himself, which is the foundation upon which all his other rights are built. It is high-handed robbery of Jehovah; for He has declared, "All souls are *mine.*" For myself, I believe there are hundreds of thousands at the South, who do *not* hold their slaves, by any means, as much "for purposes of gain," as they do from *the lust of power:* this is the passion that reigns triumphant there, and those who do not know this, have much yet to learn. Where, then, is the similarity in our views?

I forbear for the present, and subscribe myself,

Thine, but not in the bonds of gospel Abolitionism,

A. E. Grimké

LETTER II. IMMEDIATE EMANCIPATION

Brookline, Mass. 6th month, 17th, 1837

Dear Friend: Where didst thou get thy statement of what Abolitionists mean by immediate emancipation? I assure thee, it is a novelty. I never heard any abolitionist say that slaveholders "were physically unable to emancipate their slaves, and of course are not bound to do it," because in some States there are laws which forbid emancipation. This is truly what our opponents affirm; but *we* say that all the laws which sustain the system of slavery are unjust and oppressive—contrary to the fundamental principles of morality, and, therefore, null and void.

We hold, that all the slaveholding laws violate the fundamental principles of the Constitution of the United States. In the preamble of that instrument, the great objects for which it was framed are declared to be "to establish justice, to promote the *general* welfare, and to secure the blessings of *liberty* to us and to our posterity." The slave laws are flagrant violations of these fundamental principles. Slavery subverts justice, promotes the welfare of the *few* to the manifest injury of the many, and robs thousands of the *posterity* of our forefathers of the blessings of liberty. This cannot be denied, for Paxton, a Virginia slaveholder, says, "the *best* blood in Virginia flows in the veins of slaves!" Yes, even the blood of a Jefferson. And every southerner knows, that it is a common thing for the *posterity of our forefathers* to be sold on the vendue tables of the South. *The posterity of our fathers* are advertised in American papers as runaway slaves. Such advertisements often contain expressions like these: "has sometimes passed himself off as a *white* man,"—"has been mistaken for a *white* man,"—"*quite white*, has *straight* hair, and would not readily be taken for a slave," &c.

Now, thou wilt perceive, that, so far from thinking that a slaveholder is bound by the *immoral* and *unconstitutional* laws of the Southern States, *we* hold that he is solemnly bound as a man, as an American, to *break* them, and that *immediately* and openly; as much so, as Daniel was to pray, or Peter and John to preach—or every conscientious Quaker to refuse to pay a militia fine, or to train, or to fight. *We* promulgate no such time-serving doctrine as that set forth by thee. When *we* talk of immediate emancipation, we speak that we do mean, and the slaveholders understand us, if thou dost not.

Here, then, is another point in which we are entirely at variance, though the *principles* of abolitionism are "generally adopted by our opposers." What shall I say to these things, but that I am glad

thou hast afforded me an opportunity of explaining to thee what *our principles* really are? for I apprehend that *thou* "hast not been sufficiently informed in regard to the feelings and opinions" of abolitionists.

It matters not to me what meaning "Dictionaries or standard writers" may give to immediate emancipation. My Dictionary is the Bible; my standard authors, prophets and apostles. When Jehovah commanded Pharaoh to "let the people go," he meant that they should be *immediately emancipated.* I read his meaning in the judgments which terribly rebuked Pharaoh's repeated and obstinate refusal to "let the people go." I read it in the *universal* emancipation of near 3,000,000 of Israelites in *one awful night.* When the prophet Isaiah commanded the Jews "to loose the bands of wickedness, to undo the heavy burdens, and to let the oppressed go free, and that ye break every yoke," he taught no gradual or partial emancipation, but *immediate, universal emancipation. . . .*

If our fundamental principle is right, that no man can rightfully hold his fellow man as *property,* then it follows, of course, that he is bound *immediately* to cease holding him as such, and that, too, in *violation of the immoral and unconstitutional laws* which have been framed for the express purpose of "turning aside the needy from judgment, and to take away the right from the poor of the people, that widows may be their prey, and that they may rob the fatherless." Every slaveholder is bound to cease to do evil *now,* to emancipate his slaves *now.*

Dost thou ask what I mean by emancipation? I will explain myself in a few words. 1. It is "to reject with indignation, the wild and guilty phantasy, that man can hold *property* in man." 2. To pay the laborer his hire, for he is worthy of it. 3. No longer to deny him the right of marriage, but to "let every man have his own wife, and let every woman have her own husband," as saith the apostle. 4. To let parents have their own children, for they are the gift of the Lord to *them,* and no one else has any right to them. 5. No longer to withhold the advantages of education and the privilege of reading the Bible. 6. To put the slave under the protection of equitable laws.

Now, why should not *all* this be done immediately? Which of these things is to be done next year, and which the year after? and so on. *Our* immediate emancipation means, doing justice and loving mercy *to-day*—and this is what we call upon every slaveholder to do.

I have seen too much of slavery to be a gradualist. I dare not, in view of such a system, tell the slaveholder, that "he is physically unable to emancipate his slaves." I say *he is able* to let the oppressed go free, and that such heaven-daring atrocities ought to *cease now,* henceforth and forever. Oh, my very soul is grieved to find a northern woman thus "sewing pillows under all armholes," framing and fitting soft excuses for the slaveholder's conscience, whilst with the same pen she is *professing* to regard slavery as a sin. "An open enemy is better than such a secret friend."

Hoping that thou mayest soon be emancipated from such inconsistency, I remain until then,

Thine *out* of the bonds of Christian Abolitionism,

A. E. Grimké

LETTER V. CHRISTIAN CHARACTER
OF ABOLITIONISM

Newburyport, 7th month, 8th, 1837

Dear Friend: As an Abolitionist, I thank thee for the portrait thou hast drawn of the character of those with whom I am associated. They deserve all thou hast said in their favor; and I will now endeavor to vindicate those "men of pure morals, of great honesty of purpose, of real benevolence and piety," from some objections thou hast urged against their measures.

"Much evidence," thou sayest, "can be brought to prove that the character and measures of the Abolition Society are not either peaceful or christian in tendency, but that they are in their nature calculated to generate party spirit, denunciation, recrimination, and angry passion." Now I solemnly ask thee, whether the character and measures of our holy Redeemer did not produce exactly the same effects? Why did the Jews lead him to the brow of the hill, that they might cast him down headlong; why did they go about to kill him; why did they seek to lay hands on him, if the tendency of his measures was so very *pacific?* Listen, too, to his own declaration: "I came not to send peace on earth, but a sword;" the effects of which, he expressly said, would be to set the mother against her daughter, and the daughter-in-law against her mother-in-law. The rebukes which he uttered against sin were eminently calculated to produce "recriminations and angry passions," in all who were determined to *cleave* to their sins; and they did produce them even against "him who did no sin, neither was guile found in his mouth." He was called a wine-bibber, and a glutton, and Beelzebub, and was accused of casting out devils by the prince of the devils. Why, then, protest against our measures as *unchristian,* because they do not smooth the pillow of the poor sinner, and lull his conscience into fatal security? The truth is, the efforts of abolitionists have stirred up the *very same spirit* which the efforts of *all thoroughgoing* reformers have ever done; we consider it a certain proof that the truths we utter are sharper than any two edged sword, and that they are doing the work of conviction in the hearts of our enemies. If it be not so, I have greatly mistaken the character of Christianity. I consider it pre-eminently aggressive; it waits not to be assaulted, but moves on in all the majesty of Truth to *attack* the strongholds of the kingdom of darkness, carries the war into the enemy's camp, and throws its fiery darts into the midst of its embattled hosts. Thou seemest to think, on the contrary, that Christianity is just such a weak, dependent, puerile creature as thou hast described woman to be. In my opinion, thou hast robbed both the one and the other of all their true dignity and glory. Thy descriptions may suit the prevailing christianity of this age, and the general character of woman; and if so, we have great cause for shame and confusion of face.

I feel sorry that thy unkind insinuations against the christian character of Wm. Lloyd Garrison have rendered it necessary for me to speak of him individually, because what I shall feel bound to say of him may, to some like thyself, appear like flattery; but I must do what justice seems so clearly to call for at my hands. Thou sayest that "though he professes a belief in the christian religion, he is an avowed opponent of most of its institutions." I presume thou art here alluding to his views of the ordinances of baptism and the Lord's supper, and the Sabbath. Permit me to remind thee, that in *all* these opinions, he coincides entirely with the Society of Friends, whose views of the Sabbath never were so ably vindicated as by his pen: and the insinuations of hypocrisy which thou hast thrown out against him, may with just

as much truth be cast upon *them*. The Quakers think that these are not *christian* institutions, but thou hast assumed it without any proof at all. Thou sayest farther, "The character and spirit of *this man* have for years been exhibited in the Liberator." I have taken that paper for two years, and therefore understand its character, and am compelled to acknowledge, that harsh and severe as is the language often used, I have never seen any expressions which *truth* did not warrant. The abominations of slavery *cannot* be otherwise described. I think Dr. Channing exactly portrayed the character of brother Garrison's writings when he said, "That deep feeling of evils, which is *necessary* to *effectual* conflict with them, which marks *God's most powerful messengers to mankind, cannot* breathe itself in soft and tender accents. The deeply moved soul *will* speak strongly, and *ought* to speak strongly, so as to move and shake nations." It is well for the slave, and well for this country, that such a man was sent to sound the tocsin of alarm before slavery had completed its work of moral death in this "hypocritical nation." Garrison began that discussion of the subject of slavery, which J. Q. Adams declared in his oration, delivered in this town on the 4th inst. "to be the only safety-valve by which the high pressure boiler of slavery could be prevented from a most fatal explosion in this country;" and as a Southerner, I feel truly grateful for all his efforts to redeem not the slave only, but the *slaveholder,* from the polluting influences of such a system of crime.

In his character as a man and a Christian, I have the highest confidence. The assertion thou makest, "that there is to be found in that paper, or *any thing else, any* evidence of his possessing the peculiar traits of Wilberforce, (benignity, gentleness and kind heartedness, I suppose thou meanest,) not even his warmest admirers will maintain," is altogether new to me; and I for one feel ready to declare, that I have never met in any one a more lovely exhibition of these traits of character. . . .

In much haste, I remain thy friend,

A. E. *Grimké*

LETTER VIII. VINDICATION

OF ABOLITIONISTS

Groton, Mass., 6th month, 1837

Dear Friend: . . . As to Cincinnati having been chosen as the city in which the Philanthropist should be published after the retreat of its editor from Kentucky, thou hast not been "sufficiently informed," for James G. Birney pursued exactly the course which *thou* hast marked out as the most prudent and least offensive. He edited his paper at New Richmond, in Ohio, for nearly three months before he went to Cincinnati, and did not go there until the excitement appeared to have subsided.

And so, thou thinkest that abolitionists are accountable for the outrages which have been committed against them; they are the tempters, and are held responsible by God, as well as the tempted. Wilt thou tell me, who was responsible for the mob which went with swords and staves to take an innocent man before the tribunals of Annas and Pilate, some 1800 years ago? And who was responsible for the uproar at Ephesus, the insurrection at Athens, and the tumults at Lystra and Iconium? Were I a mobocrat, I should want no better excuse than thou hast furnished for such outrages. Wonderful indeed, if, in free America, her citizens cannot *choose* where they will erect their literary institutions and presses, to advocate the self-evident truths of our Declaration of Independence! And still more wonderful, that a New England woman should, *after years of reflection,* deliberately write a book to condemn the advocates of liberty, and plead excuses for a relentless prejudice against her colored brethren and sisters, and for the persecutors of those, who, according to the opinion of a *Southern* member of Congress, are prosecuting "the *only plan* that can ever overthrow slavery at the South." I am glad, *for thy own sake,* that thou hast exculpated abolitionists from the charge of the "deliberate intention of fomenting illegal acts of violence." Would it not have been still better, if thou hadst spared the remarks which rendered such an explanation necessary?

I find that thou wilt not allow of the comparison often drawn between the effects of christianity on the hearts of those who obstinately rejected it, and those of. abolitionism on the hearts of people of the present day. Thou sayest, "Christianity is a system of *persuasion,* tending by kind and gentle influences to make men *willing* to leave their sins." Dost thou suppose the Pharisees and Sadducees deemed it was very *kind* and *gentle* in its influences, when our holy Redeemer called them "a generation of vipers," or when He preached that sermon "full of harshness, uncharitableness, rebuke and denunciation," recorded in the xxiii. chapter of Matthew? . . .

Our view of the doctrine of expediency, thou art pleased to pronounce "wrong and very pernicious in its tendency." Expediency is emphatically the doctrine by which the children of this world are wont to guide their steps, whilst the rejection of it as a rule of action exactly accords with the divine injunction, to "walk by faith, *not* by sight." Thy doctrine that "the wisdom and rectitude of a given course depend entirely on the *probabilities of success*," is not the doctrine of the Bible. According to this principle, how absurd was the conduct of Moses! What probability of success was there that he could move the heart of Pharaoh? None at all; and thus did *he* reason when he said, "Who am *I*, that I should go unto Pharaoh?" And again, "Behold, they will not believe *me*, nor harken unto my voice." The *success* of Moses's mission in persuading the king of Egypt to "let the people go," was not involved in the duty of obedience to the divine command. Neither was the success of Isaiah, Jeremiah, and others of the prophets who were singularly *unsuccessful* in their mission to the Jews. All who see the path of duty plain before them, are bound to walk in that path, end where it may. They then can realize the meaning of the Apostle, when he exhorts Christians to cast all their burden on the Lord, with the promise that He would sustain them. This is walking by *faith*, not by sight. In the work in which abolitionists are engaged, they are compelled to "walk by faith;" they feel called upon to preach the truth in season and out of season, to lift up their voices like a trumpet, to show the people their transgressions and the house of Jacob their sins. The *success* of this mission, *they* have no more to do with, than had Moses and Aaron, Jeremiah or Isaiah, with that of theirs. Whether the South will be saved by Anti-Slavery efforts, is not a question for us to settle —and in some of our hearts, the *hope of its salvation has utterly gone out*. All nations have been punished for oppression, and why should ours escape? Our light, and high professions, and the age in which we live, convict us not only of enormous oppression, but of the vilest hypocrisy. It may be that the rejection

of the truth which we are now pouring in upon the South, may be the final filling up of their iniquities, just previous to the bursting of God's exterminating thunders over the Sodoms and Gomorrahs, the Admahs and Zeboims of America. The *result* of our labors is hidden from our eyes; whether the preaching of Anti-Slavery truth is to be a savor of life unto life, or of death unto death to this nation, we know not; and we have no more to do with it, than had the Apostle Paul, when he preached Christ to the people of his day.

If American Slavery goes down in blood, it will but verify the declarations of those who uphold it. A committee of the North Carolina Legislature acknowledged this to an English Friend ten years ago. Jefferson more than once uttered his gloomy forebodings; and the Legislators of Virginia, in 1832, declared that if the opportunity of escape, through the means of emancipation, were rejected, "though they might *save themselves*, they would rear their posterity to the business of the dagger and the torch." I have myself known several families to leave the South, solely from a fear of insurrection; and this twelve and fourteen years ago, long before any Anti-Slavery efforts were made in this country. And yet, I presume, *if* through the cold-hearted apathy and obstinate opposition of the North, the South should become strengthened in her desperate determination to hold on to her outraged victims, until they are goaded to despair, and if the Lord in his wrath pours out the vials of his vengeance upon the slave States, why then, Abolitionists will have to bear all the blame. Thou hast drawn a frightful picture of the final issue of Anti-Slavery efforts, as thou are pleased to call it; but none of these things move me, for with just as much truth mayest thou point to the land of Egypt, blackened by God's avenging fires, and exclaim, "Behold the issue of Moses's mission." Nay, verily! See in that smoking, and blood-drenched house of bondage, the consequences of oppression, disobedience, and an obstinate rejection of truth, and light, and love. What had Moses to do with those judgment plagues, except to lift his rod? And if the South soon finds her winding sheet in garments rolled in blood, it will *not* be because of what the North has told her, but because, like impenitent Egypt, she hardened her heart against it, whilst the voices of some of her own children were crying in agony, "O! that thou hadst known, even thou, in this thy day, the things which belong to thy peace; but now they are hid from thine eyes."

Thy friend,
A. E. Grimké

LETTER X. "THE TENDENCY OF THE AGE TOWARDS EMANCIPATION" PRODUCED BY ABOLITION DOCTRINES

. . . Thou seemest to think that the North has *no right* to rebuke the South, and assumest the ground that Abolitionists are the enemies of the South. We say, we have the right, and mean to exercise it. I believe that every northern Legislature has a right, and ought to use the right, to send a solemn remonstrance to every southern Legislature on the subject of slavery. Just as much right as the South has to send up a remonstrance against our free presses, free pens, and free tongues. Let the North follow her example; but, instead of asking her to enslave her subjects, entreat her to *free* them. The South may pretend *now,* that we have no right to interfere, because it suits her convenience to say so;

but a few years ago, (1820), we find that our Vice President, R. M. Johnson, in his speech on the Missouri question, was amazed at the "cold insensibility, the eternal apathy towards the slaves in the District of Columbia," which was exhibited by *northern* men though they had ocular demonstrations of slavery. *Then* the South wondered *we did not interfere with slavery*—and *now* she says we have no right to interfere.

I find, on the 57th p. a false assertion with regard to Abolitionists. After showing the folly of our rejecting the worldly doctrine of expediency, so excellent in thy view, thou then sayest that we say, the reason why we do not go to the South is, that we should be murdered. Now, if there are any halfhearted Abolitionists, who are thus recreant to the high and holy principle of "Duty is ours, and events are God's," then I must leave such to explain their own inconsistences; but that this is the reason assigned by the Society, as a body, I never have seen nor believed. So far from it, that I have invariably heard those who understood the principles of the Anti-Slavery Society best, *deny* that it was a duty to go to the South, *not* because they would be killed, but because the *North was guilty,* and therefore ought to be labored with *first.* They took exactly the same view of the subject, which was taken by the southern friend of mine to whom I have already alluded. "Until northern women, (said she,) do their duty on the subject of slavery, *southern* women cannot be expected to do theirs." I therefore utterly deny this charge. Such may be the opinion of a few, but it is not and cannot be proved to be a principle of action in the Anti-Slavery Society. The fact is, we need no excuse for not going to the South, so long as the North is as deeply involved in the guilt of slavery as she is, and as blind to her duty.

One word with regard to these remarks: "Before the Abolition movements commenced, both northern and southern men expressed their views freely at the South." This, also, I deny, because, as a southerner, *I know* that *I* never could express my views freely on the abominations of slavery, without exciting anger, even in professors of religion. It is true, "the *dangers, evils* and *mischiefs* of slavery" could be, and were discussed at the South and the North. Yes, we might talk as much as we pleased about *these,* as long as we viewed slavery as a *misfortune* to the *slaveholder,* and talked of "the dangers, evils and mischiefs of slavery" to *him,* and pitied *him* for having had such a "sad inheritance entailed upon him." But could any man or woman ever "express their views freely" on the SIN of slavery at the South? I say, never! Could they express their views freely as to the dangers, mischiefs and evils of slavery to the *poor suffering slave?* No, never! It was only whilst the *slaveholder* was regarded as *an unfortunate sufferer,* and sympathized with *as such,* that he was willing to talk, and be talked to, on this "delicate subject." Hence we find, that as soon as *he* is addressed as a *guilty oppressor,* why then he is in a phrenzy of passion. As soon as we set before him the dangers, and evils, and mischiefs of slavery to *the down-trodden victims of his oppression,* O then! the slaveholder storms and raves like a maniac. Now look at this view of the subject: as a southerner, I know it is the only correct one.

With regard to the discussion of "the subject of slavery, in the legislative halls of the South," if thou hast read these debates, thou certainly must know that they did not touch on the SIN of slavery at all; they were wholly confined to "the dangers, evils and mischiefs of slavery" to the *unfortunate slaveholder*. What did the discussion in the Virginia legislature result in? In the *rejection of every* plan of emancipation, and in the passage of an act which they believed would give additional permanency to the institution, whilst it divested it of its dangers, by removing the free people of color to Liberia; for which purpose they voted $20,000, but took very good care to provide, "that no slave to be thereafter emancipated should have the benefit of the appropriation," so fearful were they, lest masters might avail themselves of this scheme of expatriation to manumit their slaves. The Maryland scheme is altogether based on the principle of banishment and oppression. The colored people were to be "got rid of," for the benefit of their lordly oppressors—*not* set free from the noble principles of justice and mercy to *them.* If Abolitionists have put a stop to all *such* discussions of slavery, I, for one, do most heartily rejoice at it. The fact is, the South is enraged, because we have exposed her horrible hypocrisy to the world. We have torn off the mask, and brought to light the hidden things of darkness.

Thy Friend,
A. E. Grimké

Wendell Phillips: PHILOSOPHY OF THE ABOLITION MOVEMENT

Aroused when he heard the attorney general of Massachusetts expressing satisfaction at the death of Elijah Lovejoy, Wendell Phillips (1811–1884) thereupon launched a career of vitriolic oratory against slavery and those willing to tolerate it. His course deeply offended most of his fellow Boston patricians. Phillips was loyal to William Lloyd Garrison in the internal divisions of the abolitionist movement, but he did not agree with all Garrisonian positions, notably not with non-resistance. When Garrison urged dissolution of the American Anti-Slavery Society in 1865, Phillips became its president and continued to agitate on behalf of Negroes. He entered many other reform movements during the post-Civil War years. The following extracts from one of Phillips's many addresses to Boston abolitionists present a summary and justification of the course followed by advocates of immediatism. The speech has the tone of one vindicated, since by 1852 antislavery measures were widely embraced by political and religious leaders who had scorned them in the 1830s.

IN 1831, Mr. Garrison commenced a paper advocating the doctrine of immediate emancipation. He had against him the thirty thousand churches and all the clergy of the country,—its wealth, its commerce, its press. In 1831, what was the state of things? There was the most entire ignorance and apathy on the slave question. If men knew of the existence of slavery, it was only as a part of picturesque Virginia life. No one preached, no one talked, no one wrote about it. No whisper of it stirred the surface of the political sea. The Church heard of it occasionally, when some colonization agent asked [for] funds to send the blacks to Africa. Old school-books tainted with some antislavery selections had passed out of use, and new ones were compiled to suit the times. Soon as any dissent from the prevailing faith appeared, every one set himself to crush it.

The pulpits preached at it; the press denounced it; mobs tore down houses, threw presses into the fire and the stream, and shot the editors; religious conventions tried to smother it; parties arrayed themselves against it. Daniel Webster boasted in the Senate, that he had never introduced the subject of slavery to that body, and never would. Mr. Clay, in 1839, makes a speech for the Presidency, in which he says, that to discuss the subject of slavery is moral treason, and that no man has a right to introduce the subject into Congress. Mr. Benton, in 1844, laid down his platform, and he not only denies the right, but asserts that he never has and never will discuss the subject. Yet Mr. Clay, from 1839 down to his death, hardly made a remarkable speech of any kind, except on slavery. Mr. Webster, having indulged now and then in a little easy rhetoric,

From Wendell Phillips, *Speeches, Lectures, and Letters* (Boson: Lee and Shepard, 1894), pp. 148–53.

as at Niblo's and elsewhere, opens his mouth in 1840, generously contributing his aid to both sides, and stops talking about it only when death closes his lips. Mr. Benton's six or eight speeches in the United States Senate have all been on the subject of slavery in the Southwestern section of the country, and form the basis of whatever claim he has to the character of a statesman, and he owes his seat in the next Congress somewhat, perhaps, to antislavery pretensions! The Whig and Democratic parties pledged themselves just as emphatically against the antislavery discussion,—against agitation and free speech. These men said: "It sha'n't be talked about, it won't be talked about!" These are *your statesmen!*—men who understand the present, that is, and mould the future! The man who understands his own time, and whose genius moulds the future to his views, he is a statesman, is he not? These men devoted themselves to banks, to the tariff, to internal improvements, to constitutional and financial questions. They said to slavery: "Back! no entrance here! We pledge ourselves against you." And then there came up a humble printer-boy, who whipped them into the traces, and made them talk, like Hotspur's starling, nothing BUT slavery. He scattered all these gigantic shadows,—tariff, bank, constitutional questions, financial questions,—and slavery, like the colossal head in Walpole's romance, came up and filled the whole political horizon! [Enthusiastic applause.] Yet you must remember he is not a statesman; he is a "fanatic." He has no discipline . . . ; he does not understand the "discipline that is essential to victory"! This man did not understand his own time,—he did not know what the future was to be,—he was not able to shape it, —he had no "prudence,"—he had no

"foresight"! Daniel Webster says, "I have never introduced this subject, and never will,"—and died broken-hearted because he had not been able to talk enough about it. Benton says, "I will never speak of slavery," and lives to break with his party on this issue! Mr. Clay says it is "moral treason" to introduce the subject into Congress, and lives to see Congress turned into an antislavery debating-society, to suit the purpose of one "too powerful individual"!

These were statesmen, mark you! Two of them have gone to their graves covered with eulogy; and our national stock of eloquence is all insufficient to describe how profound and far-reaching was the sagacity of Daniel Webster! Remember who it was that said, in 1831, "I am in earnest,—I will not equivocate,—I will not excuse,—I will not retreat a single inch,—*and I will be heard!*" [Repeated cheers.] That speaker has lived twenty-two years, and the complaint of twenty-three millions of people is, "Shall we never hear of anything but slavery?" [Cheers.] I heard Dr. Kirk, of Boston, say in his own pulpit, when he returned from London,—where he had been as a representative to the "Evangelical Alliance,"—"I went up to London, and they asked me what I thought of the question of immediate emancipation. They examined us all. Is an American never to travel anywhere in the world but men will throw this troublesome question in his face?" Well, it is all HIS fault [pointing to Mr. Garrison]. [Enthusiastic cheers.]

Now, when we come to talk of statesmanship, of sagacity in choosing time and measures, of endeavor, by proper means, to right the public mind, of keen insight into the present and potent sway over the future, it seems to me that the Abolitionists, who have taken—whether for good or for ill, whether to their discredit or to their praise—this country by the four corners, and shaken it until you can hear nothing but slavery, whether you travel in railroad or steamboat, whether you enter the hall of legislation or read the columns of a newspaper,—it seems to me that such men may point to the present aspect of the nation, to their originally avowed purpose, to the pledges and efforts of all your great men against them, and then let you determine to which side the credit of sagacity and statesmanship belongs. Napoleon busied himself, at St. Helena, in showing how Wellington ought not to have conquered at Waterloo. The world has never got time to listen to the explanation. Sufficient for it that the Allies entered Paris. In like manner, it seems hardly the province of a defeated Church and State to deny the skill of measures by which they have been conquered.

It may sound strange to some, this claim for Mr. Garrison of a profound statesmanship. Men have heard him styled a mere fanatic so long, that they are incompetent to judge him fairly. "The phrases men are accustomed," says Goethe, "to repeat incessantly, end by becoming convictions, and ossify the organs of intelligence." I cannot accept you, therefore, as my jury. I appeal from Festus to Cæsar; from the prejudice of our streets to the common sense of the world, and to your children.

Every thoughtful and unprejudiced mind must see that such an evil as slavery will yield only to the most radical treatment. If you consider the work we have to do, you will not think us needlessly aggressive, or that we dig down unnecessarily deep in laying the foundations of our enterprise. A money power of two thousand millions of dollars, as the prices of slaves now range, held by a small body of able and desperate men; that body raised into a political aristocracy by special constitutional provisions; cotton, the product of slave labor, forming the basis of our whole foreign commerce, and the commercial class thus subsidized; the press bought up, the pulpit reduced to vassalage, the heart of the common people chilled by a bitter prejudice against the black race; our leading men bribed, by ambition, either to silence or open hostility;—in such a land, on what shall an Abolitionist rely? On a few cold prayers, mere lip-service, and never from the heart? On a church resolution, hidden often in its records, and meant only as a decent cover for servility in daily practice? On political parties, with their superficial influence at best, and seeking ordinarily only to use existing prejudices to the best advantage? Slavery has deeper root here than any aristocratic institution has in Europe; and politics is but the common pulse-beat, of which revolution is the fever-spasm. Yet we have seen European aristocracy survive storms which seemed to reach down to the primal strata of European life. Shall we, then, trust to mere politics, where even revolution has failed? How shall the stream rise above its fountain? Where shall our church organizations or parties get strength to attack their great parent and moulder, the Slave Power? Shall the thing formed say to him that formed it, Why hast thou made me thus? The old jest of one who tried to lift himself in his own basket, is but a tame picture of the man who imagines that, by working solely through existing sects and parties, he can destroy slavery. Mechanics say nothing but an earthquake strong enough to move all Egypt, can bring down the Pyramids.

Experience has confirmed these views.

The Abolitionists who have acted on them have a "short method" with all unbelievers. They have but to point to their own success, in contrast with every other man's failure. To waken the nation to its real state, and chain it to the consideration of this one duty, is half the work. So much we have done. Slavery has been made the question of this generation. To startle the South to madness, so that every step she takes, in her blindness, is one step more toward ruin, is much. This we have done. Witness Texas and the Fugitive Slave Law. To have elaborated for the nation the only plan of redemption, pointed out the only exodus from this "sea of troubles,"

is much. This we claim to have done in our motto of IMMEDIATE, UNCONDITIONAL EMANCIPATION ON THE SOIL. The closer any statesmanlike mind looks into the question, the more favor our plan finds with it. The Christian asks fairly of the infidel, "If this religion be not from God, how do you explain its triumph, and the history of the first three centuries?" Our question is similar. If our agitation has not been wisely planned and conducted, explain for us the history of the last twenty years! Experience is a safe light to walk by, and he is not a rash man who expects success in future from the same means which have secured it in times past.

III. THE CASE OF JOHN BROWN'S RAID

Louis Ruchames: JOHN BROWN IN THE AMERICAN TRADITION

The following essay, originally intended to introduce a collection of writings by and about the myth-laden figure of John Brown, is more than a biographical summary. It presents in detail evidence to justify actions usually regarded as at least tarnishing Brown's heroic stature. Louis Ruchames, a vigorous spokesman for the relevance of the antislavery struggle in our times, has written Race, Jobs and Politics: The Story of FEPC. *In addition to* A John Brown Reader, *he has edited* The Abolitionists: A Collection of Their Writings. *A chaplain at Amherst and Smith Colleges and the University of Massachusetts, he has also lectured and taught at these institutions.*

IT IS A hundred years since John Brown was hanged at Charlestown, Virginia on December 2, 1859, for his attack on Harpers Ferry. Perry Miller, in his study of Jonathan Edwards, refers to Harpers Ferry as a part of "the symbolism of America." As a symbol, Brown's desperate attack upon Harpers Ferry on Sunday night, October 16, 1859, has had different and frequently contradictory meanings for different groups. To the slaveholder and his sympathizers, both North and South, it was a criminal and murderous attack upon an institution sanctioned by law and justified by an ideology which regarded slavery as part of the very nature of things, with the white man born to rule and the Negro to serve. Brown was therefore a murderer and criminal who sought "to incite slaves to murder helpless women and children." His courageous behavior at his trial and execution was no more worthy of veneration than the similar behavior of any criminal. "Pirates have died as resolutely as martyrs," said the Baltimore *American*. "If the firmness displayed by John Brown proves anything, the composure of a Thug, dying by the cord with which he had strangled so many victims, proves just as much."

To many Southerners, the attack was an earnest of what could and would happen, multiplied tenfold, under a government not totally committed to a defense of slavery. The thought of a possible Republican victory in the forthcoming election of November, 1860, when seen by Southerners in the context of Harpers Ferry, caused almost hysterical alarm. In the Senate, during the following January, Robert Toombs counseled his people, "Never permit this Federal government to pass into the hands of the black Republican party. It has already declared war against you and your institutions. It every day commits acts of war against you: it has already compelled you to arm for your defence. . . . Defend yourselves! The enemy is at

Reprinted from *A John Brown Reader*, edited by Louis Ruchames, by permission of Abelard-Schuman, Ltd., pp. 11–32. All rights reserved.

your door, wait not to meet him at your hearthstone; meet him at the doorsill, and drive him from the Temple of Liberty, or pull down its pillars and involve him in a common ruin."

On the other hand, in Northern antislavery circles, Brown represented the highest idealism: the willingness to sacrifice one's life and possessions for the freedom and welfare of one's fellow men. In a lecture on November 8, 1859, in Boston, Emerson referred to Brown as "The Saint, whose fate yet hangs in suspense, but whose martyrdom, if it shall be perfected, will make the gallows as glorious as the Cross." In an address delivered in Concord almost two weeks after Harpers Ferry, Thoreau remarked that "when I think of him, and his six sons, and his son-in-law, not to enumerate the others, enlisted for this fight, proceeding coolly, reverently, humanely to work, for months, if not years . . . without expecting any reward but a good conscience, while almost all America stood ranked on the other side,—I say again, that it affects me as a sublime spectacle." Thoreau indeed anticipated his friend Emerson in comparing Brown to Jesus. "Some eighteen hundred years ago Christ was crucified; this morning, perchance, Captain Brown was hung. These are the two ends of a chain which is not without its links. He is not Old Brown any longer; he is an angel of light." Wendell Phillips, who had devoted the previous twenty-five years to the anti-slavery movement, went so far as to regard Harpers Ferry as the beginning of emancipation. Invoking Brown as "marvellous old man," he said: "History will date Virginia Emancipation from Harper's Ferry. True, the slave is still there. So, when the tempest uproots a pine on your hills, it looks green for months,— a year or two. Still, it is timber, not a tree. John Brown has loosened the roots of the slave system; it only breathes,— it does not live,—hereafter."

Few events in American history provide so vivid an illustration of the thesis that the historian's evaluations of men and events are dependent not upon facts alone but upon the basic premises from which he views those facts. It is his "inarticulate major premises," as Oliver Wendell Holmes aptly put it, that determine his judgments. In the case of Brown, the determining factor in all judgments, whether of the ordinary citizen or the scholar, was one's attitude toward slavery. To those who regarded slavery as "the sum of all villainies," as legalized kidnapping maintained by jails, the lash, and, ultimately, the death penalty for those who sought to secure their freedom or to help others do so, Brown's action was one of great idealism and placed him in the company of the great liberators of mankind. Theodore Parker, the great Unitarian clergyman and Abolitionist, expressed this point of view as ably and frankly as anyone, in a letter to Francis Jackson, an outstanding anti-slavery leader in Boston. "A man held against his will as a slave," he wrote, "has a natural right to kill every one who seeks to prevent his enjoyment of liberty. The freeman has a natural right to help the slaves recover their liberty, and in that enterprise to do for them all which they have a right to do for themselves." After asserting the duty of one man to help another get rid of a wolf or a murderer in case of an attack, he asks: "Suppose it is not a murderer who would kill you, but a kidnapper who would enslave, does that make it less my duty to help you out of the hands of your enemy? Suppose it is not a kidnapper who would make you a bondman, but a slaveholder who would keep you one, does that remove my obligation to help you?" In the light of these opinions one can well appreciate Parker's final judgment that "there have been few spirits more pure and devoted than John Brown's, and none that gave up their breath in a nobler cause. Let the American State hang his body, and the American Church damn his soul; still, the blessing of such as are ready to perish will fall on him, and the universal justice of the Infinitely Perfect God will take him welcome home. The road to heaven is as short from the gallows as from a throne; perhaps, also, as easy." Even men like Garrison, who were non-resistants, and did not themselves wish to use force to achieve freedom for the slave, cheered Brown's effort as a valid alternative to continued slavery. "Rather than see men wearing their chains in a cowardly and servile spirit," he said at a meeting memorializing Brown, "I would, as an advocate of peace, much rather see them breaking the head of the tyrant with their chains. Give me, as a non-resistant, Bunker Hill, and Lexington, and Concord, rather than the cowardice and servility of a Southern slave-plantation."

Those whose opposition to slavery was only lukewarm, whose dislike of the institution led them to oppose its extension but was not sufficiently strong to cause them to strive for its elimination in the South, condemned Brown's attack and accepted his execution as justified. But they too saw a certain element of nobility in his character and behavior. Samuel J. Kirkwood, Governor of Iowa, expressed this point of view, which was shared by many, when he said: "While the mass of our people utterly condemn the act of John Brown, they feel and they express admiration and sympathy for the disinterestedness of purpose by which they believe he was governed,

and for the unflinching courage and calm cheerfulness with which he met the consequences of his failure."

The conflict of ideologies has continued to our own day. The grandson of William Lloyd Garrison, Oswald Garrison Villard, a man of broad humanitarian sympathies, who has written the definitive biography of Brown, concludes his study with this observation, "The story of John Brown will ever confront the spirit of despotism, when men are struggling to throw off the shackles of social or political or physical slavery. His own country, while admitting his mistakes without undue palliation or excuse, will forever acknowledge the divine that was in him by the side of what was human and faulty, and blind and wrong. It will cherish the memory of the prisoner of Charlestown in 1859 as at once a sacred, a solemn and an inspiring American heritage."

In opposition to this point of view stands James Malin,[1] the foremost anti-Brown historian, who seems unable to forgive the North for having used force against Southern secession, or the Abolitionists for having taught that the abolition of slavery would be a step forward for American society, or the Negro for having believed that his welfare would be furthered by the forceful elimination of slavery. To Malin, minor errors of date or place committed by writers who have a high regard for Brown are frequently labeled deliberate falsehoods, while the errors of Brown-haters are simply unintentional blunders. Very few anti-slavery leaders and writers emerge unscathed under Malin's furious onslaught. Typical of his method are his comments on Emerson, Thoreau, Parker

[1] James C. Malin, *John Brown and the Legend of Fifty-Six* (Philadelphia: American Philosophical Society, 1942), 794 pp.

and the other leaders of New England opinion, whom he contemptuously refers to as the "New England Transcendental Hierarchy, the self-appointed keepers not only of New England culture, but, according to their own estimates, of national civilization." Following in the footsteps of earlier anti-Brown biographers, such as Hill Peebles Wilson and Robert Penn Warren, Malin refers to the sympathetic evaluation of Brown as "the John Brown legend," a "hoax" created largely by the above-mentioned "hierarchy." To expose the "hoax," he concludes, would result in breaking "the spell of its authority" and deflating "other fakes and fakers" as well. Malin has accumulated a wealth of facts in his volume and thereby has induced many historians to accept his point of view, but a closer examination of the book reveals many errors of fact,[2] and an approach which, though it claims to be scientific, is notably lacking in the dispassionate objectivity of the true scientist.

The purpose of this volume is not, however, the examination of all that has been written about John Brown, whether pro or con, or its evaluation from the point of view of historical accuracy. It is intended, rather, to present the positive impact of John Brown upon American thought, viewing his life and death as events which evoked great idealism as well as some of the noblest and most memorable writing in the history of American letters.

We approach this task from the point of view of those who believe that the struggle against slavery and its elimination during the Civil War was one of the great positive achievements in American history; that the Abolitionists and other anti-slavery leaders, who devoted their lives to the achievement of freedom for the slave and equality of opportunity for Negro and white alike, seeking through their writings and lectures to educate the American public to the evils of slavery, were not paranoiacs or narrow-minded fanatics, but men and women who were devoted to the highest ideals of equality and democracy, influenced by the best in the Judaeo-Christian tradition and all that was good and noble in the thoughts and actions of the Founding Fathers. John Brown was one of this company of anti-slavery men. This anthology, by presenting the John Brown tradition, seeks to contribute to a firmer understanding of one of the vital aspects of American history, as well as to help our own generation, in a small way, toward a greater appreciation of those very ideals which motivated Brown and his friends.

JOHN BROWN'S LIFE IN BRIEF

John Brown was born on May 9, 1800, in Torrington, Connecticut, the second son of Owen and Ruth Mills Brown. According to family tradition, the Browns were descended from Peter Brown of the Mayflower through Peter Brown of Windsor, Connecticut, who was pre-

---

[2] For example, on pp. 4–5, one finds at least eight errors in the reproduction of a letter from John Brown to his father. In other parts of the book, names are misspelled and key phrases omitted from documents. It is important to note that in the reconstruction of the events leading to the Pottawatomie killings in Kansas, the reminiscences of members of the Brown family are arbitrarily excluded. Furthermore, the book is based almost exclusively on the materials available in the files of the Kansas State Historical Society. The important collections of John Brown material owned by other state historical societies, the Library of Congress, college libraries, and authorities on John Brown such as Boyd B. Stutler and Dr. Clarence S. Gee are either not used at all or only in a very limited way.

sumed to be the former's son.[3] Both of John Brown's grandfathers fought in the American Army during the Revolution. His mother, Ruth Mills Brown, was descended from Dutch settlers who had come to this country during the seventeenth century. His father, Owen, an anti-slavery man even before John Brown's birth, and an agent of the Underground Railroad, was a God-fearing Congregationalist, who earned a livelihood as farmer, shoemaker and tanner.

In 1805, Owen Brown moved his family to Hudson, Ohio. There John received his education, and grew up as a hard-working, pious and disciplined young man. In the spring of 1816, John made a formal profession of religion and was accepted into the Congregational church at Hudson. Deciding to enter the ministry, with the intention of ultimately preparing for it at Amherst college, he went East with his brother, Salmon, and a friend, Orson Oviatt, and enrolled at a school conducted by the Rev. Moses Hallock in Plainfield, Mass. He stayed there only a few months and transferred in the winter of 1816–17, with his brother and friend, to Morris Academy, near Litchfield, Conn. Litchfield was then, according to Boyd B. Stutler, an "abolition and anti-slavery center, birthplace of Harriet Beecher Stowe, and home of many other nota-

bles." Because of an inflammation of the eyes and a lack of funds, John was forced to give up his studies and return home, resuming his work at his father's tannery in Hudson.

At the age of twenty he married Dianthe Lusk, the plain-looking, pious and amiable daughter of a widow who lived near the Brown homestead, whose maiden name was Mary Adams[4] and who traced her ancestry back to the renowned Adams family of Massachusetts. Six years later they moved to Randolph (now New Richmond), Pennsylvania, with their three children, John, Jr., Jason and Owen—there were to be four more children, only two of whom, Ruth and Frederick, were to live to maturity.

The years from 1826 to 1835 were filled with business successes and noteworthy achievements in commercial leadership. Ernest A. Miller, in a pamphlet entitled "John Brown, Pennsylvania Citizen,"[5] has dwelt upon the events of those years. Brown cleared twenty-five acres of land; built a tannery, a log house and a barn—which included a carefully concealed room to hide fugitive slaves escaping to Canada and elsewhere; organized a school for his own children and those of a neighbor; formed a church, which he served as clerk; and helped establish a post office in Randolph, which he served as postmaster. His success as a cattle breeder was notable, his tannery prospered, employing at times as many as fifteen men, and he was generally recognized and looked up to as a valuable member of the community.

This period has justifiably been de-

---

[3] Oswald Garrison Villard, in his biography of John Brown, denied that Peter Brown of Windsor was the son of Peter Brown of the Mayflower. His opinion was based on the researches of several genealogists. Donald Lines Jacobus, editor-in-chief of *The American Genealogist*, has recently re-evaluated all the known facts in the case and has come to the same conclusion. (See his "Peter Brown of Windsor, Conn." in *The American Genealogist*, XXXIII [October, 1957], 214–222.) However, Dr. Clarence S. Gee, of Lockport, New York, probably the foremost living student of the Brown family genealogy, maintains the validity of the family tradition.

[4] I am indebted to Dr. Clarence S. Gee for this name. Previous biographers do not mention it.
[5] Published by the Pennsylvania State Press, Warren, Pa., 1952. 27 pp.

scribed as "the most peaceful and prosperous period in the nearly sixty years of his turbulent life."[6] But it was not without its sorrows. In March, 1831, Brown's four-year-old son, Frederick, died and in August, 1832, Brown's wife, Dianthe, thirty-one years old, died a few hours after the death of a new-born infant son. About a year later, Brown remarried, taking as his wife Mary Ann Day, the daughter of a blacksmith who lived fifteen miles from New Richmond. Brown's second wife bore him thirteen children, of whom seven died in childhood and two were slain at Harpers Ferry.

In 1835, attracted by new business opportunities, especially the offer of a partnership in tanning with Zenas Kent, a successful businessman, Brown moved his family to Franklin Mills (now Kent), Portage County, Ohio. The partnership did not materialize but Brown involved himself in land speculation, utilizing, for the most part, borrowed funds. With the onset of the depression of 1837, his speculations failed, leaving him deeply in debt for the rest of his life.

From 1837 to 1844, he tried various sources of income—tanning, breeding race horses, raising sheep, and buying and selling cattle. With none of these did he succeed in recouping his fortune. In fact, so great had his poverty become that, at one point, he turned to his personal use $2800.00 which had been given him for the purchase of wool by the New England Woolen Company, at Rockville, Conn., through its agent, George Kellogg. Fortunately, the company had no desire to prosecute him and it accepted his pledge to pay the amount in install-

ments, as circumstances would permit. (In 1859, in his last will and testament, Brown bequeathed fifty dollars toward payment of the remainder of his debt.)

His fortunes reached their lowest ebb in 1842, when he was forced into bankruptcy and emerged stripped of almost all his possessions. For years afterwards he was plagued with lawsuits by creditors. To cap his misfortunes, he lost four children, aged nine, six, three and one, in an epidemic during the following year.

In spite of his financial reverses, Brown's reputation for industry and integrity remained intact and in 1844 he entered into a business partnership—the last of his career—with Simon Perkins, a wealthy businessman of Akron, Ohio, whose flock of sheep Brown was to manage. He moved his family from Richfield, Ohio, where they had been living since 1842, to Akron, and there they remained for the next two years. In 1846, the two partners opened an office and wool depot in Springfield, Mass., for the purpose of disposing of wool for Western wool-growers. Brown was placed in charge. Although the wool-growers showed their enthusiasm for the new company's plans by sending in large quantities of wool, the resistance of the wool manufacturers and uncertain business conditions placed the firm in difficulties almost from the beginning. Brown was unable to sell the wool at profitable prices, and although he undertook a trip to Europe, from August to October 1849, to sell the wool abroad, his effort failed disastrously and he returned to a business that was in greater difficulties than ever before. In 1850 it had to be abandoned entirely. Brown retired to Akron, partly to continue farming and sheep-raising in partnership with Perkins, and partly to carry the burden of a

[6] Boyd B. Stutler in a Radio Broadcast entitled "Old John Brown of Osawatomie," a chapter in *The American Story*, Number: AS-84, 1956.

multiplicity of lawsuits resulting from their business failure.

Whatever may be said of Brown's lack of business ability, his failure as a businessman in Springfield did not prevent him from achieving an enviable reputation for integrity and honesty. In December, 1859, at a public meeting in Northampton, Mass., held several days after Brown's hanging, Thomas Musgrave, a wool manufacturer of Northampton, who had bought heavily from Perkins & Brown, had this to say of Brown: "I never saw a man more upright in all his dealings than he was. I saw him after he had lost every dollar, and he remarked to me that he was thankful to God that he was yet alive. Men were willing to trust everything in his hands. There was not a man that he ever dealt with that could say that he had ever wronged them out of a single penny. I will say to you, ladies and gentlemen, that whatever he said could be depended upon."[7]

During his years in Springfield, Brown had involved himself increasingly in anti-slavery activities. According to Frederick Douglass, the Negro anti-slavery leader, who visited Brown in Springfield in 1847, Brown attributed the meager furnishings of his home and his rather primitive manner of living to his efforts to save money for a project involving the forceful liberation of slaves. Toward the end of 1847 or the first half of 1848, Brown wrote an essay entitled "Sambo's Mistakes," for *The Ram's Horn*, a Negro newspaper published in New York, in which he urged Negroes to show a more vigorous resistance to their oppressors. In 1851, he organized among the Negroes of Springfield a League of Gileadites, whose purpose it was to resist attempts under the recently enacted

Fugitive Slave law to capture fugitive slaves and return them to slavery.

Previously, his desire to help the Negroes induced him to move his family in 1849 from Springfield, where they had been living since 1847, to North Elba, New York, for two years. This step resulted from an offer made in 1846 by Gerrit Smith, of Peterboro, New York, an outstanding anti-slavery philanthropist and political figure, to give one hundred and twenty thousand acres of land in northern New York to Negroes for settlement. Brown decided that he wanted to settle with his family among them "to aid them by example and precept." He purchased 244 acres of farmland from Smith and, until such time as he could erect his own house, rented a farmhouse near North Elba, into which he moved his family in 1849. In spite of Brown's assistance, the Negro settlement at North Elba failed. Brown, beset by numerous lawsuits following the failure of his business in Springfield in 1850, and under an obligation to continue the farming and sheep-raising part of his partnership with Simon Perkins, moved back to Akron, Ohio, with his family, in 1851.

The return to Akron was originally conceived by Brown as a temporary measure. He planned to remain there and to continue working with Perkins only as long as it would take to terminate their partnership and to wind up their affairs. This took longer than expected, but by 1854 the partnership of Perkins and Brown came amicably to an end. By then Brown had accumulated sufficient funds to enable him to transport his family back to North Elba, where they moved into an unplastered four-room house built for them by Henry Thompson, Ruth Brown's husband, who had previously set up housekeeping with Ruth in North Elba. It was there that the

---

[7] *The Hampshire Gazette* (Northampton, Mass.), December 6, 1859.

Browns were still living when John Brown was executed in 1859.

The return to North Elba marks a turning point in Brown's life. Thereafter, he gave up all thoughts of business and devoted himself entirely to the struggle against slavery; first, as a guerrilla leader in Kansas and then in preparation for his attack upon Harpers Ferry.

The passage of the Kansas-Nebraska Act in May, 1854, which provided that the issue of slavery in Kansas and Nebraska was to be decided by the residents of those territories, set off a contest between North and South, with both sides making every effort to pour men and money into the Territory to assure control. John Brown's children, Owen, Frederick and Salmon, dissatisfied with their circumstances in Ohio and eager to lend a helping hand to the forces of freedom in Kansas, left Ohio for Kansas in October, 1854, and arrived there the following spring. They were joined in May by Jason and John, Jr., who arrived with their families. They settled eight miles from Osawatomie, where their uncle, Rev. Samuel Lyle Adair, had settled the previous year. Although in 1854 John Brown had no intention of accompanying his children to Kansas, he seems to have changed his mind at the beginning of 1855. When, in May of that year, he received a letter from John, Jr., stressing an urgent need for arms, he decided to leave for Kansas as soon as possible with whatever arms he could secure. He purchased arms with funds raised at a number of anti-slavery meetings, and arrived in Kansas in October, 1855, accompanied by his son-in-law, Henry Thompson, and his son, Oliver.

Kansas was at the time in the grip of a reign of terror unloosed by pro-slavery Missourians and other Southerners determined on making the Territory safe for slavery. The following remarks by one Missourian leader in a speech at St. Joseph, Missouri, in March, 1855, indicate the policy being pursued: "I tell you to mark every scoundrel among you that is the least tainted with free-soilism, or abolitionism, and exterminate him. Neither give nor take quarter from the d - - - d rascals. . . . To those having qualms of conscience, as to violating laws, state or national, the time has come when such impositions must be disregarded, as your lives and property are in danger, and I advise you one and all to enter every election district in Kansas, in defiance of Reeder and his vile myrmidons, and vote at the point of the bowie-knife and revolver. Neither give nor take quarter, as our cause demands it. It is enough that the slave-holding interest wills it, from which there is no appeal."[8]

Such advice was implemented by a liberal use of tar and feathers, beatings, murders and attacks upon the homes and crops of Free-State men. Periodically, hordes of armed Missourians would invade the Territory at election time, vote for pro-slavery candidates and return to their homes. One invasion took place in November, 1854, when upward of a thousand armed Missourians crossed into Kansas, voted for a pro-slavery delegate to Congress, and returned home. A second occurred in March, 1855, when at least five thousand men in armed companies crossed into Kansas, voted for a pro-slavery legislature, stuffed ballot boxes and terrorized anti-slavery voters and officials. The legislature they helped to elect proceeded to enact a code of

[8] Quoted in Sara T. Robinson, *Kansas: Its Interior and Exterior Life* (Boston, 1857), pp. 14–15. Andrew T. Reeder was the first territorial governor of Kansas.

laws which Oswald Garrison Villard has called "one of the foremost monuments of legislative tyranny and malevolence in the history of this country,"[9] and which a pro-slavery leader in Kansas praised as being "more efficient to protect slave property than those of any state in the Union."[10] Only pro-slavery men could hold office or serve as jurors; it was a felony punishable by at least two years' imprisonment to deny the legality of slavery in Kansas, or even to discuss whether slavery in Kansas "exists or does not exist," and death was the penalty for creating dissatisfaction among slaves or inciting them to conspire or rebel.

In effect, not only was slavery thenceforth legal in Kansas but no effort could be made, through democratic methods of expression and assembly, to eliminate it. Such efforts were illegal and punishable by imprisonment and even death. To make matters worse, "every sheriff and probate judge, as well as every other county officer in the Territory was an appointee of the bogus Legislature and a Pro-Slavery man. There were no Free-State officers."[11] The panoply of the law constituted a shield for every violent and lawless pro-slavery action, and an additional means of terror against those who refused to surrender their anti-slavery beliefs.

The months following John Brown's arrival in Kansas, in the fall of 1855, were spent by Brown and his sons in building homes, contending with illness, battling freezing temperatures, attending meetings of Free-State settlers and defending the anti-slavery cause. Those months were also marked by a resurgence of violence, slayings of three Free-State settlers within three months, an invasion of Kansas and a threatened attack upon Lawrence in December. Brown and four sons joined other Free-State men in going to the defense of Lawrence. Fortunately, warfare was averted through a last-minute agreement between the Free-State leaders of Lawrence and Wilson Shannon, the pro-slavery Governor of Kansas.

The remaining months of winter were quiet, but this period was, in the words of Charles Robinson, a Free-State leader and later Governor of Kansas, "one of preparation." The onset of spring witnessed new invasions by desperadoes from Missouri, Georgia and Alabama, arrests and attempted arrests of Free-State leaders on charges of treason—punishable by imprisonment and even death —and further killings of Free-State men. These culminated in a descent upon Lawrence on May 20 and 21, by a "swearing, whiskey-drinking, ruffianly horde,"[12] under the command of a United States Marshal, I. B. Donaldson, for the ostensible purpose of serving writs of arrest against a number of Free-State leaders who had been indicted for "constructive treason" by a pro-slavery grand jury. This same grand jury had recommended the abatement of two Free-State newspapers published in Lawrence and of the Free State Hotel in the same city. As a result, several citizens of the city were arrested on charges of treason; the two newspaper offices destroyed; their presses, books and papers thrown into the river; the Free State Hotel bom-

[9] *John Brown: A Biography Fifty Years After* (New York: Alfred A. Knopf, 1943), p. 91.
[10] Quoted in George Martin, "The First Two Years of Kansas," *Kansas State Historical Society Collections*, X, 132.
[11] Address by Honorable T. Dwight Thacher, *Kansas State Historical Society Collections*, III, 443.

[12] James Ford Rhodes, *History of the United States* (New York, 1904), II, p. 158. Quoted in Villard, *John Brown*, p. 145.

barded by cannon and set afire; and the home of Charles Robinson razed.

John Brown and his sons, with others from their area, were on their way to the relief of Lawrence when they were met by a messenger on May 22, who informed them of the attack. Outraged by the news, as well as by previous depredations and killings—two young antislavery men named John Jones and John Stewart had been killed just prior to the attack on Lawrence—and disgusted by the timid refusal of Free-State leaders to defend themselves from the repeated outrages, Brown decided upon a reprisal which has come to be known as the Pottawatomie killings. On May 23, the day after receiving the news about Lawrence, he led a group of seven men, including his sons Owen, Frederick, Salmon, and Oliver, his son-in-law, Henry Thompson, and two others, Theodore Wiener and James Townsley, to the Pottawatomie settlement. On the night of May 24, at midnight, Brown and his men took from their cabins five pro-slavery men who had actively aided the invaders, defended the pro-slavery cause and threatened Free-State settlers in their area, and killed them with broadswords. Although Brown himself did not do any of the killing, he was the leader of the group and was undoubtedly responsible for the conception and execution of the deed.

Contemporary historians have tended to condemn Brown for the killing. At the time it occurred, the Free-State settlers of Kansas took a more sympathetic view of the matter. Judge James Hanway, a leading settler, had this to say in 1878 concerning the attitudes of the settlers in 1856 and later:

". . . So far as public opinion in the neighborhood, where the affair took place, is concerned, I believe I may state

that the first news of the event produced such a shock that public opinion was considerably divided; but after the whole circumstances became known, there was a reaction in public opinion and the Free State settlers who had claims on the creek considered that Capt. Brown and his party of eight had performed a justifiable act, which saved their homes and dwellings from threatened raids of the pro-slavery party."[13] There is no doubt that if one judges the killings in isolation from other events of the day, the resulting judgment will be one of condemnation. However, if they are placed within their historical context, a different view will tend to emerge. What must have been Brown's state of mind on the night of the killings was expressed in a dispatch from Leavenworth, Kansas, on May 20, which appeared in the New York *Daily Tribune* on May 30, 1856: "No man's life is safe; no kind of property secure. A Guerrilla war exists in Kansas, and unless the people in the States come to our rescue and relief speedily, we shall all likewise perish." Brown, instead of supinely waiting for help from outside the Territory, took matters into his own hands.

Further insight into the situation is given by two hitherto unpublished letters. One is by Rev. Samuel Lyle Adair, John Brown's brother-in-law, as mild and decent a person as one could find in the Territory; the other, by his wife Florilla. Writing on May 16, 1856, Florilla Adair tells of the fear of death with which the Free-State settlers in and near Osawatomie lived. "It is believed that Osawatomie is in danger any day or night. You ask in one of your letters if we have any fear of our lives. I think now we are constantly exposed and we

[13] Ms. by James Hanway in Kansas Historical Society. Quoted in Villard, *op. cit.*, p. 170.

have almost no protection. . . . A few
have their guns and revolvers, but as a
people and place we are without even
these and the place is known and called
an *abolition nest.* . . ."[14]

The letter by Rev. Samuel Adair was
written several days after the Pottawatomie killings.[15] It expresses what must
also have been the reaction of many of
Adair's neighbors: that the killings, as re-
prisals, were a hopeful sign of resistance
to the pro-slavery terror. The letter first
refers to a previous one in which the attack on Lawrence had been described.
It then continues:

.I now add that the houses of citizens
were entered, money, arms, & goods at the
peril of life were demanded. And in this
way the citizens were robbed of about
Fifty Thousand Dollars in money, arms,
& goods. Horses & cattle, etc., etc., were
taken; & not only was this done in Lawrence, but also by guerilla parties that
went in different directions among the
people of the country.

But, it has been found that gun which
they have been firing is beginning to kick,
& it is not certain whether it will not produce greater terror, & do more execution
at the brick [breech] than it has yet done
at the mussle [muzzle].

The assassination of Jones a few weeks
ago was a mere flash in a pan, or the bursting of a cap, as an experiment to see what
the effect would be. You will recollect the
murder of Dow last November—of Barber
in Dec., of Brown in Jan., of Jones & Stew-
ard, last week; or a thousand other outrages. Five Free State men shot or butch-
ered: not only did not [sic] did bogus
authority refuse to lift a finger to bring to
justice these murderers, but has shielded
them. The U.S. territorial officers have done

the same. Now what is the result? Guerilla
parties are now forming & organizing
through all the territory. A descent was
made by one party on Saturday night last
& five pro-slavery men were shot or butch-
ered in one night. Some of them had made
threats, had threatened the lives of Free
State men—had acted most outrageously
for some time past—they probably were
dreaming of no danger to themselves. Some
of them were taken from their beds and
almost literally hewed to peices [sic] with
broad swords. The scene of these desperate
deeds, is only about eight miles from us.
The excitement produced has been most
tremendous. Money, arms, horses, etc. were
taken. Some pro-slavery men took the
alarm & fled—many free state also left their
houses for a few nights. Runners were sent
to Missourie, for help.—And pro-slavery
men in different localities gathered together
or stood in fear of their lives. Missourie
troops have not come and it is thought they
will not come in large numbers and it is
well for them not to. But if they do, they
may expect to find one of their party dead
when they return, a house burnt, a horse
stolen, as the case may be when they return. As many pro-slavery men must die
as free state men are killed by them, and
they will not be particular who he is, so he
is one who has made himself officious in
Kansas matters. "Eye for eye, tooth for
tooth"—dollar for dollar & compound interest in some cases may be demanded.

There is much reason to believe that
John B. Sen. & sons—J-jun, & Jason ex-
cepted, who were with the company en-
camped near the Santa Fe road at the time
of the transaction—were with the company
that did the deed, John & Jason have been
taken & are now before court at Batteeses—
8 miles from here—. An effort was made to
take Owen, but did not succeed. John &
Jason can be proved clear of any participa-
tion in the act by more than one hundred
men. Yet we know not what will be done
with them. Their wives and children are
with us. The rest of the men, are armed to
the teeth & out some where, we know not

[14] Copy in the Villard Collection, Columbia
University Library. The letter is addressed to
"Dear Sister Martha."
[15] Copy in the Villard Collection, Columbia
University Library. It is addressed to "Dear
Bro. & Sis. Hand & Other Friends."

where. Pro-slavery men are in terror, for if this is the beginning of the discharges of a gun they have been shooting when turned the other way they know not what the end will be.

During the ensuing months, Brown and his men went into hiding, but Jason and John, Jr., who had not participated in the killings, were captured by pro-slavery forces and Federal troops and imprisoned. They were later released, Jason in June and John in September. In the meantime, John Brown's reputation as a guerrilla leader grew. On June 2, he defeated and captured a force of twenty-three pro-slavery men headed by Henry Clay Pate, a captain in the Missouri militia, deputy United States Marshal and newspaper correspondent. At the end of August, he fought a skirmish at Osawatomie in which he led a band of thirty or forty men against two hundred and fifty commanded by a Mexican War veteran, John W. Reid. Though badly outnumbered, Brown fought back hard and succeeded in escaping with the bulk of his force. Prior to the engagement, his son, Frederick, had been killed by the vanguard of Reid's force, and afterward, Osawatomie itself was burned. Brown participated in other guerrilla engagements, but by the fall of 1856, under the vigorous administration of a new Governor, John W. Geary, much of the warfare had ceased and conditions in Kansas grew relatively quiet. Feeling that he was no longer needed, Brown decided to return East. Henry Thompson, Oliver and Salmon, fed up with the fighting and killing, had left in August and at the beginning of October, Brown, with John, Jr., Jason and Owen crossed over from Kansas to Iowa.

As he left Kansas, Brown was carrying a letter from Charles Robinson, a Free-State leader and first Governor of Kansas. About two decades after Brown's death, Robinson turned into a mortal enemy of Brown's memory, but in 1856, he wrote the following:[16]

Lawrence, Sept 15, 1856

Capt. John Brown: My Dear Sir:—I take this opportunity to express to you my sincere gratification that the late report that you were among the killed at the battle of Osawatomie is incorrect.

Your course, so far as I have been informed, has been such as to merit the highest praise from every patriot, and I cheerfully accord to you my heartfelt thanks for your prompt, efficient and timely action against the invaders of our rights and the murderers of our citizens. History will give your name a proud place on her pages, and posterity will pay homage to your heroism in the cause of God and Humanity.

Trusting that you will conclude to remain in Kansas and serve during the war the cause you have done so much to sustain, and with earnest prayers for your health and protection from the shafts of Death that so thickly beset your path, I subscribe myself,

> Very respectfully
> Your Ob't Servant
> C. Robinson

It was at the beginning of 1857 that Brown reached Boston. He met the city's outstanding philanthropists, scholars and anti-slavery leaders, and impressed them with his abilities as a leader of men and with his sincerity and devotion to the anti-slavery cause. During his stay in Boston and other Eastern cities he succeeded in enlisting the moral and financial support of a secret committee of men who served as his devoted backers during the ensuing years. These were Gerrit Smith, Dr. Samuel G. Howe,

[16] Printed in Villard, *op. cit.*, pp. 262–3.

Thomas Wentworth Higginson, George L. Stearns, Theodore Parker and Franklin B. Sanborn. However, in 1857, their knowledge of his plans included only future forays in Kansas. It was not until the following year that they learned of the projected attack in Virginia.

In March, 1857, in New York, Brown met Hugh Forbes, a British soldier-of-fortune, who had fought under Garibaldi in Italy. Impressed by his knowledge and ability, Brown hired Forbes to train recruits for service in Kansas and Virginia. Ultimately, Forbes proved a greater hindrance than help. He broke with Brown in 1858, when the plan for the attack on Virginia had already matured, and then threatened to publicize the entire scheme. As a result, Brown was forced to postpone his plans for an entire year.

Brown spent a good part of the spring and summer of 1857 in raising funds for future campaigns in Kansas, and at the beginning of November he was back in the Territory. But he found little to do there. Conditions had quieted considerably, the Free-State settlers had scored significant successes at the polls, and Governor Robert J. Walker of Mississippi, who had succeeded Governor Geary, seemed sincerely interested in preventing fraudulent voting. Brown left Kansas before the end of November, but not before he had made another important decision: to launch the attack on Harpers Ferry as soon as possible. By the time he left Kansas, he had already enlisted ten recruits, including his son Owen.

He brought his men to Springdale, Iowa, found quarters for them and then headed East to meet with his supporters and to secure their financial help. He spent three weeks with Frederick Douglass in Rochester, visited with Gerrit Smith, Sanborn and others in Peterboro, New York, saw Higginson, Parker, Howe, Sanborn and Stearns in Boston, and spent some time in Canada, where he visited St. Catherine's, Ingersoll, Chatham and Toronto, and met many leaders of the Negro communities. He decided to hold a convention of his followers at Chatham, returned to Springdale where he gathered his men and brought them back to Chatham.

The convention opened on May 8, 1858. Present were Brown's party of twelve, including himself, and thirty-five Negroes. To allay suspicion, it was announced that the purpose of the convention was to organize a Masonic lodge among Negroes. The presiding officer was Rev. William Charles Munroe, pastor of a Detroit Negro church; the secretary, John H. Kagi, was later killed at Harpers Ferry. The proceedings included an address by Brown, in which he presented his plans, the adoption of a "Provisional Constitution and Ordinances for the People of the United States," and the election of officers.

Brown's plan, apparently, was to move from the convention to the point of attack in Virginia. But he had not reckoned on the intervention of Forbes. While the convention was yet in session it was learned that Forbes had revealed the substance of the plans to certain political leaders. Brown's backers, with the exception of Higginson, were terrified and demanded that the entire project be abandoned for the time being. Brown acceded to their demands and directed his steps toward Kansas, re-entering the territory at the end of June, where he lived under the name of Shubel Morgan. He spent most of his time in southeastern Kansas, where James Montgomery, a Free-State guerrilla leader, had been operating. Brown's most famous exploit while there was a foray into Missouri, on December 20, where he and his men forcefully liberated eleven Negro slaves, brought them safely to Canada—a distance of eleven hundred miles—in eighty-two days, with the authorities constantly on their heels and a price of $250.00 on Brown's head.

As the spring of 1859 approached, the fears occasioned by Forbes's revelations subsided, and Brown felt ready for the move which had been his ultimate goal for twenty years. He rented the Kennedy Farm in Maryland, at the beginning of July, used it as a base for preparations, and on the night of October 16 set out with eighteen of his men—leaving three behind at the farm—to capture Harpers Ferry. Harpers Ferry was chosen because within it were located a United States Armory and Arsenal, which could provide arms for the numerous slaves who were expected to flock to Brown's standard. The town was taken without difficulty, but Brown delayed unnecessarily. By Monday afternoon he was surrounded by the Virginia militia and escape became impossible. On Tuesday morning, the doors of the engine house in which Brown and his surviving men had taken refuge were battered down by U. S. Marines under the command of Colonel Robert E. Lee, and the battle was over.

The raid had proven a failure. The slaves had not been liberated nor did they rise to assist those who sought to free them. Of the twenty-two men comprising the "Army of Liberation," five escaped, ten were killed and seven, including Brown, captured and hanged later. Other casualties included seven dead—a free Negro, two slaves, a Marine and three white citizens—and ten wounded.

Brown was brought to trial on October 25, a week after capture, and was found guilty six days later of three crimes: conspiring with slaves to rebel, murder and treason. Though his lawyers sought to enter a plea of insanity on the basis of affidavits received from residents of Ohio, he rejected the attempts and refused to permit any such plea. Concerning the trial itself, Richard B. Morris, the well-known historian, notes that it was "flagrantly unfair."

The right of the accused to a reasonable time to prepare for trial was shockingly violated. Brown was forced to stand trial the very same day he was indicted. Scrupulous though the court was to provide the accused with competent trial counsel, it erroneously denied him the right to engage lawyers of his own choice. When, finally, his own counsel took over, they were given no time to familiarize themselves with the case against their client.

To this catalogue of judicial errors must be added a last one: John Brown was tried and sentenced for a crime of which he could not conceivably have been guilty. How the accused could have committed treason against Virginia when he was neither a citizen nor a resident of that state and owed it no allegiance was never clarified by the law enforcement authorities. Objectivity and reason gave way to hysteria and vigilantism. This was no time for technicalities. It was enough that John Brown be convicted of a crime carrying the capital penalty and that the sentence of the court be carried out with expedition.[17]

Morris also suggests that Brown should have been examined by an alienist or psychiatrist, and implies that if he had been, he might never have been brought to trial. As has just been indicated, efforts were made during the trial

[17] Richard B. Morris, *Fair Trial* (New York: Alfred A. Knopf, 1953), pp. 259–260.

to have him adjudged insane. On the second day of the trial Brown's lawyer received a telegram from A. H. Lewis of Akron, Ohio, editor of the *Summit Beacon*, emphasizing that insanity was hereditary in Brown's family on his mother's side. After the trial, in a further attempt to secure clemency, nineteen affidavits, gathered by one of Brown's lawyers from relatives and friends in Ohio, repeated the same information and added that Brown was insane on the subject of slavery. At one point, Governor Wise issued an order to have Brown examined by an alienist, but then countermanded the order.

As to whether Brown was or was not insane, the best answer lies in an examination of his behavior at the trial and afterward. Certainly, his remarks and actions at the trial show no indication of insanity, nor has it ever been alleged that they do. His speech to the court before sentence was pronounced is regarded by many as one of the finest utterances in American literature; Emerson, indeed, compared it in later years to Lincoln's Gettysburg address. His letters from prison are models of lucidity and breathe a rare nobility of thought and character. "No lunatic," writes Villard, "ever penned such elevated and high-minded, and such consistent epistles."[18] Brown's concentration upon slavery and its evils throughout the latter part of his life, which is the usual reason given for alleging his insanity, was indeed intense and unusual for his day. But it was not unusual when compared to that of such men and women as William Lloyd Garrison, Wendell Phillips, Lydia Maria Child, Theodore Parker, Charles Sumner, Maria Weston Chapman and Parker Pillsbury, to name but a few,

who devoted their lives to the anti-slavery cause, suffered hardships and privations for its sake, and at various occasions were also accused of being fanatics and insane on the subject of slavery. The lesson to be learned from their example is simply that to be deeply sensitive to injustice, to be willing to devote one's life to an unpopular cause, to give up the pursuit of one's own gain to alleviate the suffering of others, involves running the risk of being called fanatic and even insane by the smug, the callous and the well-placed members of society. "The prophet is a fool, the man of the spirit is mad!" has echoed through the ages, from the days of Hosea to our own.

Finally, perhaps the most important evidence as to the nature of John Brown's mind and character is to be found in the devotion to him of the twenty-one young men—intelligent, able and high-minded—who lived with him and knew him as a leader and a friend, and who followed him even unto death.[19]

[18] *Op. cit.*, p. 509.

[19] Among recent historians, Professors C. Vann Woodward and Allan Nevins have emphasized the case for Brown's insanity. Prof. Vann Woodward has made much of the nineteen affidavits testifying to insanity in Brown's family, especially on his mother's side, and to Brown's own insanity or "monomania" on the question of slavery. Putting aside the basic question of whether one's insanity may be established by the presence or absence of insanity in one's family, it may be noted that the affidavits are highly suspect as valid evidence. Their primary purpose was to save Brown from execution by showing him to be insane. They must, therefore, be regarded not as objective reports but as partisan statements made to achieve a certain purpose, with every possibility that the material they present may be biased in the direction of proving insanity. Moreover, their reliability as evidence is weakened still further by the fact that they include significant sections which are based, quite explicitly, not on direct knowledge but on hearsay and secondhand information.

By accepting the affidavits at their face value, Prof. Vann Woodward, though a very

John Brown's end came on December 2, on a scaffold in Charlestown. His execution served as a visible demonstration by the state of Virginia of the condign punishment ultimately in store for

those who sought to tamper with the institution of slavery; for the slave seeking to escape from bondage and for the free man, white or colored, who dared to aid him.

To the North, however, Brown's execution brought a far different lesson. For in John Brown, whose venture at Harpers Ferry it first saw as the desperate act of a demented old man oblivious to the realities of the world, the North came to see the embodiment of all that was noble, courageous, and self-sacrificing in man's love for his fellow man. It saw beyond the bloodshed and death into the heart of a man who had identified himself with the poorest, the lowliest, the most forsaken people of the land, had thrown in his lot with theirs, had given up his home, his possessions, his ambitions, his wife and children whom he loved, even life itself, to bring freedom and dignity to men, women and children who had known only the bitterness and hopelessness of slavery. As they saw the state of Virginia, in all of its majesty, proceed in indecent haste to exact the life of the man who had threatened its power, the people of the North learned, as little else could have taught them, that the structure of slavery remained intact primarily through the power of the whip, the gun and the gallows and that when these were gone there was little else left. They learned, too, that wealth and happiness derived from the sweat of slaves was not less easily relinquished than that gotten through more honorable means, and that the slaveholder would fight desperately, with all the means at his disposal, to maintain the foundation of his wealth and power. It was then that many in the North realized that the issue of slavery and freedom would be decided by the

---

careful historian, is led into committing several errors. He states, for instance, that one of Brown's brothers was insane. This assertion is made in only one of the affidavits and is not substantiated by any evidence. The brother referred to was the editor of the New Orleans *Bee* and a prominent figure in New Orleans public affairs. All that we know of him indicates that he was quite sane. Prof. Vann Woodward also asserts that Brown's mother, grandmother, sister and sister's daughter were insane. Family letters and other records cast doubt upon that part of the assertion which refers to the grandmother and sister's daughter, while a careful reading of the affidavits themselves fails to reveal any reference to the insanity of Brown's mother. All available evidence affirms her sanity. One may also question Prof. Nevins' evidence, which he has assiduously gathered, in seeking to prove Brown's insanity. Since limitations of space prevent an extended analysis, the following will have to suffice. Prof. Nevins writes that Brown "was subject to extravagant religious fixations. In 1852, worried because his son John did not exhibit piety, he spent an entire month writing a letter of pamphlet length to him, composed largely of scriptural quotations. We might question the sanity of a nearly penniless man with a large family who devotes a month to such an exhortation—which proved futile." A close reading of the letter in question, which is printed in full in F. B. Sanborn's *John Brown*, pp. 45–51, reveals the very opposite of what Prof. Nevins believes it to prove. In the letter Brown writes as follows: "It is now nearly a month since I began on another page. . . . I did mean that my letter should go off at once, but I have not become very stout, and have a great deal to look after, and have had many interruptions. We have done part of our sowing, and expect to get all our corn (of which we have a good crop) secure from frost this day." Prof. Vann Woodward's discussion of Brown is in "John Brown's Private War," *America in Crisis*, ed. by Daniel Aaron (New York: Alfred A. Knopf, 1952), pp. 109–130. Prof. Nevins evaluates Brown in *The Emergence of Lincoln* (New York and London: Charles Scribner's Sons, 1950), II, 5 ff.

weapons that the South had chosen. The battle at Harpers Ferry demonstrated what those weapons were.

When the war came, almost two years later, the man who had been hanged rose, as it were, from his grave to march again with those who had finally taken up the cause for which he had fought, and, by proffering the example of his life and work, helped to achieve the victory which he had lost in life but gained in death.

Tilden G. Edelstein: JOHN BROWN AND HIS FRIENDS

Tilden G. Edelstein, who shares a warm interest in the present-day civil rights movement, disagrees sharply with Ruchames's view that Brown is a suitable hero for that movement. First presented as a lecture at Amherst College in the fall of 1962, the following essay raises important questions concerning the intentions of Brown and those abolitionists who helped him prepare for the Harpers Ferry raid. Edelstein, who teaches at Simmons College, is the author of a biography of Thomas Wentworth Higginson, one of the "Secret Six."

A VIRGINIA jury, on October 31, 1859, found John Brown guilty of murder, treason and conspiring with slaves and others to rebel. Since that time, questionable logic and the omission and distortion of historical evidence have enabled many advocates of civil rights to say that John Brown was not only innocent but also a friend of the oppressed, a hero and a martyr. His most militant antebellum allies have been similarly praised for their unselfish nobility.

The painful slowness with which Negroes are achieving their civil rights appears to re-affirm, in the minds of many friends of the Negro, the need for faith in John Brown and his fellow conspirators. For example, a writer in the May 1962 issue of *The Crisis*, the NAACP magazine, has argued that "the souls of most white Americans are too lacking in the sense of identification" with Brown.

While the hateful violence of today's Southern mobs is condemned, the violence of Brown and his supporters is viewed as humanitarian activism. The present concern for civil rights has helped to obscure the historical case against Brown and to obscure what it means to glorify the Harpers Ferry Raid.

Supporting Brown's use of violence, Henry Thoreau asserted: "The method is nothing; the spirit is all." This argument has been re-stated by one of Brown's most recent defenders, Professor Louis Ruchames, in the Introduction to his anthology, *A John Brown Reader*. He proposes that John Brown, like the other Abolitionists and the Founding Fathers, was devoted "to the highest ideals of equality and democracy" and "the best in the Judaeo-Christian tradition." That Brown frequently practiced the ruthless and relentless use of deception and violence as a means of operation is considered irrelevant, therefore, for judging Brown and his "spirit." Ruchames, in an article in the *Nation*, "The Historian as Special Pleader," suggests valuable points about the underlying convictions and historical inaccuracies of historians who have been unsympathetic to Brown, to Charles Sumner and to the Abolitionists; but he wholly ignores the comparable shortcomings of the more liberal special pleader.

The Abolitionist John Greenleaf Whittier stands as one of the few ante-bellum friends of the Negro who was unsure about the ultimate destination toward which John Brown's soul was marching. After the Harpers Ferry Raid, Whittier said: "I have just been looking at one of the *pikes* sent here by a friend in Baltimore. It is not a Christian weapon; it looks too much like murder." Later, in a poem, Whittier moved closer to praising the spirit of John Brown:

> Perish with him the folly
>   That seeks through evil, good;
> Long live the generous purpose
>   Unstained with human blood!
> Not the raid of midnight terror,
>   But the thought which underlies;
> Not the outlaw's pride of daring,
>   But the Christian sacrifice.

Neither Whittier's hesitancy nor Ruchames's affirmation can be found in Professor C. Vann Woodward's "John Brown's Private War." Woodward suggests that Brown's "doctrine that the end justifies the means had arrived pretty close to justifying the liquidation of an enemy class." Brown's defenders largely ignore this issue of separating means from ends. Though Ruchames discusses Woodward's article, he erroneously suggests that its main emphasis is Brown's insanity and that its author

agrees with Professor Allan Nevins that Brown was a monomaniac even "before he turned to slavery." Woodward, it is true, enumerates no less than twenty-one cases of permanent or temporary insanity in the Brown family tree and in another article refers to "demented John Brown." Unlike Nevins, however, he concedes that such a view rests primarily upon the affidavits collected by Brown's defense counsel to forestall a trial; and Woodward further admits that "opinion varied" as to the sanity of Brown himself.

From 1859 to the present, a teleological assumption and a belief in the inevitability of historical events have helped Brown's defenders to feel secure in separating means from ends and have also served to give the Harpers Ferry Raid a disproportionate importance. Credibility to the Civil War's inevitability has come from an historian who is no defender of Brown, and who in other writings has judged gradualism to be the habitual and normative pattern of American reform from Jackson's day through the days of the New Deal and the New Frontier. Arthur Schlesinger, Jr., has suggested that when "great moral issues" are at stake "the unhappy fact is that man occasionally works himself into a log-jam; and that log-jam must be burst by violence." Brown's supporters have readily agreed. They have relied upon the assumption that there is a purpose and design in nature that works itself out with or without the help of man: the Civil War is seen as a necessary condition for emancipation, and the Harpers Ferry Raid as a necessary condition for the outbreak of war. Too often it has been assumed with certitude that since the war ended slavery and since John Brown brought war, then it is sound history to assert, by syllogism, that John Brown deserves a place as the emancipator of the slave. Violence is judged, in retrospect, as *absolutely* the only way slavery could have ended.

Much of the praise for Brown has depended upon another kind of questionable logic, a kind which perhaps can be termed the *worth by association fallacy*. Throughout our history, men committed to a pluralistic society and to freedom of association, have fought against the repressive practice of employing the guilt by association concept to silence and condemn people with ideas and associations that correspond at certain points with those held by men far more extreme. But they have been less vigilant about the dangers of worth by association. To join with people of different views can be justified, of course, on ideological and practical grounds; but it is intellectually unsound for men to hold in uncritical high regard and to embrace as indistinguishable compeers, individuals whose ideas and associations only partly correspond with their own. This sort of weakness has had an enormous influence in raising the reputation of John Brown far beyond the level justified by his deeds. Too frequently Brown has received praise primarily because he associated with humanitarian Abolitionists and because he desired to end slavery. But the fallacy of such gratuitous praise becomes apparent if one recalls the number of demagogues, tyrants and dictators who offered their lives in the effort to bring into being what they believed to be a better society. That a man joined a group which aided runaway slaves, which spoke against slavery, or which fought against the South does not automatically make his motives idealistic, establish his contribution to these causes, nor equalize his role with all others in the group. Receiving this undeserved immunity from careful scrutiny, the story of what Brown was, said, and did, often is allowed to remain hidden behind the colorful rhetoric spun by John Brown and his defenders.

The journalist Oswald Garrison Villard, in 1910, published his *John Brown: A Biography Fifty Years After*. A heavily documented book of 738 pages, it long has been considered the most complete and accurate account of the deeds of Brown and his ante-bellum allies. A grandson of William Lloyd Garrison, the author was the son of Fanny Garrison Villard, who was a leader in American peace movements, and of Henry Villard, railroad magnate and newspaper publisher. By the time he began writing his Brown biography, Villard was an active liberal spokesman. Not only had he been an articulate pacifist since the Spanish-American War, but from 1908–1910, while completing his book, Villard led an attack against the leadership of Booker T. Washington and the policy of accommodating and appeasing Southern racism. Villard, along with Dr. W. E. B. Du Bois, sought to establish a new and active organization to fight for the civil and political rights of the Negro. His efforts led directly to the formation, in 1910, of the NAACP. Villard, Professor Flint Kellogg notes, "hoped that the celebration by the colored people of the fiftieth anniversary of John Brown's death might inspire its birth."

In the Preface to his biography Villard promised a study "free from bias . . . and from the blind prejudice of those who can see in Brown nothing but a criminal." This goal could be attained, he was sure, by putting forth "the essential truths of history." Though deploring Brown's wholesale use of violence in the chapter titled "Murder on the Pottawatomie," Villard produced a warmly sympathetic account of his life. First, he acquits Brown of criminality, and then, in his concluding chapter, "Yet Shall He Live," he suggests: "In Virginia, John Brown atoned for Pottawatomie by the nobility of his philosophy and his sublime devotion to principle even to the gallows."

Despite the author's intention to write sound history, his fight against Booker T. Washington's excessive gradualism and his commitment to pacifism appear to have led to severe omissions and distortions of the Brown tale. Seeking to condemn Washington's appeasement of Southern racism by contrasting it with Brown's militancy, while simultaneously trying to maintain his own pacifism, induced Villard to cover Brown and the Harpers Ferry raid with an heroic mantle. Upon Villard's book much of the subsequent defense of Brown has depended for its historical foundation.

No subsequent biography of Brown has appeared which has had sufficient scope to supplant Villard's heavily documented study. But manuscript sources not hitherto cited and some of the work of Professors James Malin, Allan Nevins, C. Vann Woodward and Robert Penn Warren, can be utilized to begin to set the record straight. Malin's *John Brown and the Legend of Fifty-Six* (1942) stands as the most extensive scholarly effort to confront Villard and those who before and after him have perpetuated the Brown cult. In this study of Brown in Kansas, Malin establishes that Brown hardly was known there and had little influence "either in making or marring Kansas history." He shows that "the business of stealing horses under the cloak of fighting for freedom" was both a major and a profitable enterprise for Brown and his men. Manuscripts reveal that stealing United States postage stamps

and passing a bad check for $100 were other notable, if less renumerative, parts of Brown's Kansas operations. After thirty-five years and the successive failures of most of his twenty different business enterprises, several of which, according to Malin, were marked by "flagrant dishonesty," John Brown moved into the antislavery business. Imbued with a sincere hatred of slavery, Brown acquiesced to the hard fact that monetary profits were not imminent. He appeared able to envision, however, his future elevation to Commander-in-Chief of a post-revolutionary nation shorn of slavery, which would provide him with both power and money. Entering a market where the demand for revolutionaries was modest and the supply even more modest, and understanding that the new calm in Kansas had left radical Abolitionists in a quandary about where to invest money for antislavery action, Brown displayed real entrepreneurial skill in raising resources for his projects. But he scarcely can be described as "noble and good" and possessing the "highest idealism."

His efforts to procure money and arms from that group of prominent Northerners who called themselves the Secret Six, reveal a man adept at playing upon the guilt felt by wealthy and militant abolitionists who talked of revolution but were not prepared to take part personally in the shooting. In making one of his many requests for money from Franklin B. Sanborn, a disciple of Emerson and the principal of a Concord private school, Brown suggested that Sanborn and his friends become "conscious that I am performing that service which is equally the duty of millions who need not forego a single hearty dinner by the efforts they are called on to make."

Carefully pitting his key supporters against each other to give each one the feeling of being the closest confederate, Brown wrote to one member of the Secret Six, the celebrated radical Unitarian minister, Reverend Theodore Parker, to assure him that "none of them understand my views as well as you do." Both to Parker and to another Abolitionist clergyman, Thomas Wentworth Higginson, he expressed doubt about the abolitionist earnestness of Sanborn and of another confederate, the affluent Boston manufacturer George L. Stearns. Brown did this in the face of the fact that Sanborn and Stearns were his stanchest supporters while Parker and Higginson had been skeptical about supplying large amounts of money and arms. This strategy was a major factor in increasing Brown's resources. Higginson was flattered that Brown confided to him that Stearns and Parker "overrated the obstacles," lacked "courage" and "were not men of action." Writing about Brown's way of dealing with fellow conspirators, he said: "The sly old veteran . . . appeared to acquiesce [to the others] far more than he really did. . . . But he wishes me not to tell them what he had said to me."

That Higginson called Brown "the sly old veteran" is important not only for what it discloses about a militant Abolitionist's estimate of Brown's character prior to Harpers Ferry, but also for what it reveals about Villard's biography. Higginson's statement is reprinted with the omission of the adjective "sly." Despite the great clarity of Higginson's handwriting, and though Higginson frequently was consulted during the writing of the book, the biographer still found the word "illegible." Seeking to raise the reputation of Brown to heroic heights, Villard appears to have feared that Brown's character could not be compared favorably with the martyrs of world history. And the "illegible" word has continued to elude print.

If Brown callously used and manipulated the Secret Six—and the truth of this is further indicated by his leaving behind in the Maryland farmhouse where he must have known they would be found, private papers and letters implicating his absent Northern allies—unpublished manuscripts indicate another side to the relationship between Brown and his Northern supporters. Ten days before the raid, Sanborn informed Higginson that "an eager youth" of twenty-two would come to see him. He was en route, said Sanborn, to join Brown to contribute his services along with $600 of his own gold. The arrival in Worcester of young Francis Merriam, a nephew of the Boston Abolitionist Francis Jackson, apparently shocked Higginson. Merriam was frail, was totally blind in one eye and appeared to be either mentally unbalanced or severely retarded. Earlier, Merriam had written to Wendell Phillips about a desire to give money for "stealing slaves down South" and to partake in such action. Confessing that Southerners "might kill me, of which I should be glad although I am a coward, and do not know how much I should dare do, even in that Cause," he asked Phillips: "Could poison or a deadly weapon be passed to a prisoner caught in the South for stealing slaves?"

When Higginson complained about the fitness of this recruit, Sanborn sent him a revealing letter, a letter which Villard copied from the original manuscript but chose not to mention in his book. Three days before the raid, Sanborn wrote:

'tis a virtue posted in numbskulls to give money freely. . . . I consider him about as fit to be in this enterprise as the devil is to keep a powder house; but everything has its use & must be put to it if possible.

Out of the mouths of babes and sucklings come dollars by the hundred, and what is wisdom compared to that? I do not expect much of anybody . . . but when a plum drops in your mouth shall you not eat it because it is not a peach or a pumpkin?

On October 16, John Brown invaded Virginia and within thirty-six hours was subdued by troops under the command of Brevet-Colonel Robert E. Lee. Brown's revolutionary activities now had permanently ended, but his Northern supporters still sought to use him as their expendable instrument. During the time preparations were being made for Brown's trial, Higginson wrote: "I don't feel sure that his acquittal would do half as much good as his being executed. . . ." Brown was less eager for execution. His request for legal counsel included the admonition: "Do not send an Ultra-Abolitionist."

Later, when Brown became reconciled to his fate, he had to battle against the Abolitionists' desire to send his wife to visit him in jail to gain public sympathy. He was forced to have a telegram sent North. Anticipating great expense and a painful scene, he followed this with a letter. "I . . . was feeling quite cheerful before I heard she talked of *coming* on. . . . I can certainly judge better in the matter than ANYONE ELSE." But Mrs. Brown was sent. Also, despite his firm opposition to plans to try to free him forcefully, plans were made to free him (insufficient funds prevented the attempted rescue). Even at the point of death John Brown had to strive to avoid being manipulated by his off-stage supporters. After the execution, when preparations were being made to move the body to his home at North Elba, New York, the Brown family was asked by some of these Northern conspirators to make one more sacrifice. But the Browns refused. They denied a request to move John Brown's body to a grave in Mt. Auburn Cemetery in Cambridge.

Thirty years later, Garrison's son, Wendell Phillips Garrison, confidently posed this question: "What would John Brown have been without Boston?" Whether Brown duped his Northern supporters (as Woodward has suggested) more than they used him, indeed is open to question. Certainly the relationship was less than noble. Brown freely deceived and manipulated the Secret Six. Deserving still greater emphasis, however, is that they showed few compunctions about sending him and his undermanned force to almost certain death. To Brown's eleventh-hour plea that they join him, they responded by staying home and sending Sanborn's "plum," Francis Merriam. After the raid their eagerness for self-sacrifice did not increase.

In 1943, thirty-three years after his book had first appeared, Oswald Garrison Villard published "a new and revised edition." Actually, an Addenda summarizing some manuscript material uncovered since 1910, an additional bibliography, and a new Preface were the only changes in the book. But the Preface, if not the text, showed that the author's views had been influenced by Malin's *John Brown and the Legend of Fifty-Six* and affected even more profoundly by the movement of world events since 1910. Having equally condemned Stalin and Hitler and having maintained his pacifist position, Villard —the one-time liberal reformer—turned by 1937 to support Republican conservatism and isolationism. Only after Pearl Harbor did he approve America's military efforts. Writing his Preface during the war, Villard still could praise Brown's "spirit and courage in the face of certain death," but was now greatly troubled by Brown's "resort to murderous violence and the armed revolt against his government." Unlike 1910, he said that "there were no pro-slavery crimes to justify Pottawatomie massacres. . . . Nothing could have excused Brown and his sons for taking the law into their own hands and stabbing men to death with broadswords, just when they were denouncing the pro-slavery forces for violating the Constitution and overriding the laws of their country."

Villard, however, despite new reservations about Brown's morality and despite Malin's research, would not surrender unconditionally. Writing a review of Malin's book, he argued: "But Professor Malin to the contrary notwithstanding, there must have been something in this man to seize the imagination of great sections of the American people, to stir the hearts of men like Channing, Emerson, John A. Andrew, Thomas Wentworth Higginson, Wendell Phillips, and numerous others who flowered and led in New England. Granted that his hands were blood-stained; that his business record was one succession of failures and defaults; that the amount of insanity in his family was appalling and that he received credit for many things he did not do, and was not adequately scourged for sins and crimes, he still becomes a symbol and remains an imperishable figure in our history." Says Villard in exclamation, "Surely, no man who was merely a midnight assassin and a horse-thief could have become that!"

What Villard now granted, of course, was enormous; what remained of his case was tenuous. If it is acknowledged that men often become heroic symbols and imperishable figures in history for reasons having more to do with excessive presentism, questionable logic and historical inaccuracy, than with historical fact, Villard's final argument appears to depend solely upon the reliabil-

ity of popular sentiment and upon the testimony of prominent ante-bellum character witnesses. For Villard, and for all others who have similarly defended Brown, to use such evidence as proof neglects another crucial part of the Harpers Ferry story. Warren suggested, in 1929, and even Brown's supporters generally have agreed, that the prisoner's final trial speech was pivotal in bringing many ante-bellum men to praise the life and work of John Brown. This moving speech indicated to Northerners who previously had been critical or cool to him, the high courage Brown possessed in the face of death. More important, as Warren noted, the speech denied that Brown had any intention of either spilling blood at Harpers Ferry or of fomenting a slave insurrection in the South. With fine rhetorical skill Brown dropped the role of the vengeful soldier of the Lord who sought to punish the forces of slavery and instead slipped into the garments of a merciful son of God. John Brown's execution, concluded Emerson, "will make the gallows as glorious as the cross."

But by what kind of marvelous alchemy was John Brown transformed into the Prince of Peace? That Brown, in 1858, had revealed plans for a slave insurrection in his "Provisional Constitution and Ordinances for the People of the United States"—a document reprinted in full in the 1860 Report of the Senate Investigating Committee—should have convinced more men that the raid was never intended to be merely an affair in which slaves would voluntarily join Brown, live quietly in the mountains of Virginia, and be peacefully sent on their way to Canada. Villard, in his book, seeking to reconcile his own pacifism with sympathy for Brown, explained this damning document by choosing to "lay it aside as a temporary aberration of a mind that in its other manifestations defies classification as unhinged or altogether unbalanced." How then can one reconcile peaceful intentions with Brown's collection of two hundred revolvers, two hundred rifles, and nine hundred and fifty pikes specially chosen for slaves to use in insurrection, or with his seizure of a United States arsenal, a federal armory and a rifle works? And how does one reconcile peaceful intentions with his previous Kansas record of homicide, or with his killing of four residents of Harpers Ferry, the first of whom was a Negro freeman?

Ante-bellum newspapers and manuscripts indicate that Brown's closest conspiratorial supporters played a major part in permitting men to avoid having to confront such questions. These men first helped Brown toward insurrection and then they helped to erase his deeds and theirs from the pages of history. Before the failure of the Harpers Ferry venture became apparent, they had explicitly advocated and encouraged plans for a slave insurrection. As early as May 1857 Higginson told the annual meeting of the American Anti-Slavery Society that "the question of slavery is a stern and practical one. Give us the power, and we can make a new Constitution, or we can interpret the old one. How is that power to be obtained? By politics? Never. By revolution and that alone." And in September of the same year Sanborn understood that Brown was "as ready for revolution as any other man. . . ." "I could not wonder," said Sanborn in February 1858, "if his plan contemplated an uprising of slaves. . . ." Three months later, Higginson again spoke from the public platform and this time joined the issue of insurrection with an estimate about the behavior of the Negro slave. "We white Anglo-Saxons," said this descendant of the first minister in the Massa-

chusetts Bay Colony, "are too apt to assume the whole work is ours. Behind all these years of shrinking and these long years of cheerful submission [by the slave] . . . there may lie a dagger and power to use it when the time comes. . . . We speak of the American slave as if he was never to do anything for his own emancipation." Slavery, he predicted, "is destined, as it began in blood, so to end." And when a man uninformed about Brown's plans suggested to Higginson, in late November 1858, that a new Northern organization should be formed to go South and foment insurrection, he replied that such plans already were launched, apologizing for not being "at liberty to be more explicit." But he did say that insurrection would come "by the action of the slaves themselves, in certain localities, with the aid of *secret* cooperation from the whites." While other antislavery men looked hopefully to the new Republican party which opposed the extension of slavery, Higginson said: "Had there been an insurrection every year since the American Revolution, I believe slavery would have been abolished ere this. . . . A single insurrection, with decent temporary success would do more than anything to explode our present political platforms." Finally, when the first bits of exaggerated news about the raid reached Massachusetts, he joyfully referred to "the most formidable slave insurrection that has ever occurred. . . ."

But as soon as it became apparent that Brown's assault had ended in complete disaster for the Abolitionist forces, Higginson and the other conspirators joined the retreat. Sanborn, quickly deciding to forego the opportunity to lead his Concord students in their annual chestnut-hunting excursion, fled toward the Canadian border. "According to advice of good friends and my own deliberate judgment," wrote this zealous advocate of revolution, "I am to try a change of air for my old complaint . . . , whether my absence will be long or short will depend on circumstances. . . . Burn this. . . ." Stearns and Samuel Gridley Howe joined the migration north. Frederick Douglass, who preferred to put the Atlantic Ocean between him and the federal government, fled to England. Gerrit Smith, the Syracuse philanthropist who had given Brown more money than any other man, stayed in this country but needed temporary shelter at the New York State Asylum for the Insane at Utica.

Putting the John Brown story into verse, Stephen Vincent Benét, reflecting the judgment of historians for and against Brown, wrote: "Only the tough, swart-minded Higginson/ Kept a grim decency, would not deny." And it is true that Higginson neither denied complicity nor fled the country. It has not been recognized, however, that Higginson, like all other close ante-bellum supporters of Brown except Parker (who was the only conspirator out of the country for health reasons unconnected with the Harpers Ferry epidemic), denied in another way. He would never again say that John Brown and his Northern allies had been looking forward to a slave insurrection. Instead, some forty years after the raid, Higginson claimed that he had known in 1859 that "the delicate balance of the zealot's mind" had been "somewhat disturbed."

Wendell Phillips did say that "the lesson of the hour is insurrection," but he then added: "I ought not to apply that word to John Brown of Osawatomie. . . . It is a great mistake to call him an insurgent." James Redpath, an Abolitionist journalist and a companion of both Brown and Merriam, wrote a series of newspaper articles during late October 1859 which he variously titled "Reminiscences of the Insurrection" and "Notes on the Insurrection." He categorically stated: "Brown believed that slavery must be abolished by a servile insurrection." But after Brown's final trial speech expressing abhorrence of bloodshed and insurrection, Redpath also changed his mind. He even took a step backward. His book, *The Public Life of John Brown*, published soon after Brown's death, made no mention of slave insurrection. Brown sought "not revolution but justice," wrote Redpath. The author refrained from connecting the deeds of Brown in Kansas and Brown at Harpers Ferry. "For such a notion," he shrewdly conceded in private, "degrades him from the position of a Puritan 'warring of the Lord' to a guerrilla chief of vindictive character." Brown's defenders, from Emerson to the present day, generally have been as understanding as Redpath.

Today, as in Villard's day, John Brown "the martyr" is being recruited to provide a viable tradition for the civil rights cause. Exonerated posthumously from the guilt of murder by its being compared with the greater guilt of slaveholders, he has become identified with men of good will. But it should be remembered that his ante-bellum allies hesitated about supporting him until his execution day drew near and memories of his deeds became easily blurred. And there is real doubt whether John Brown, their expendable warrior, ever identified with these men who were sure of their next "hearty dinner." It is also doubtful whether the embattled heroes of today's civil rights organizations, those with or without dinners, should imagine that John Brown, the apostle of violence, would have identified with them.

IV. THE SEARCH FOR NEW PERSPECTIVES

Avery Craven: THE NORTHERN ATTACK ON SLAVERY

*A noted advocate of the view that the Civil War was a great na-
tional tragedy, Avery Craven, of the University of Chicago, presents
his evaluation of abolitionists, especially William Lloyd Garrison, in
the following selection from his* The Coming of the Civil War *(1942).
Craven was one of the first historians to suggest psychological mal-
adjustment as a partial explanation for abolitionists' activities, and
his interpretation has been widely influential.*

REMOVING motes from a brother's eye
is an ancient practice. The urge to
make over other individuals and to correct real or fancied evils in society oper-
ates with unusual force in certain individuals. This used to be ascribed to a peculiar sensitiveness of wrongdoing—a
willingness to sacrifice personal comfort
for a larger good. Perpetual reformers,
though resented as meddlers by those
they disturbed, have been hailed as pioneers and martyrs who have unselfishly
helped to usher in new eras and a better
world.

The modern psychologist is somewhat
skeptical of such explanations. He talks
of youthful experiences, maladjustments,
inferiority complexes, and repressed
desires. He is not so sure about the
sources of the reform impulse or the unselfish character of the reformer. The
student of social affairs is likewise less
inclined to grant unstinted praise to
the fanatic and is not certain about the
value of the contribution. He views him
as a normal product of social phenom-
ena acting on certain types of personality. He sees the triumph of emotion over
reason in the extremist's course and

sometimes wonders if the developments
of history might not have been more
sound without him. He talks with less
assurance about "progress" in human affairs.

At all events, recent historians have
been inclined to reconsider the part
played by the abolitionists in the coming of the War Between the States. They
have judged the reformer and his efforts
to be open fields for new study. The old
assumptions that the movements against
slavery arose entirely from a disinter-
ested hatred of injustice and that their
results were good beyond question can
no longer be accepted without reservations. Those who force the settlement of
human problems by war can expect only
an unsympathetic hearing from the future. Mere desire to do "right" is no defense at the bar of history. . . .

The abolition movement was . . .
closely related in origins, leadership, and
expression to the peace movement, the
temperance crusade, the struggles for
women's rights, prison and Sabbath reform, and the improvement of education. It was not unrelated to the efforts to
establish communities where social-

From Avery Craven, *The Coming of the Civil War* (New York: Charles Scribner's Sons, 1942),
pp. 117–18, 134–38, 149–50. Reprinted by permission of the author.

economic justice and high thinking might prevail. It was part of the drive to unseat aristocrats and re-establish American democracy according to the Declaration of Independence. It was a clear-cut effort to apply Christianity to the American social order.

The anti-slavery effort was at first merely one among many. It rose to dominance only gradually. Fortunate from the beginning in leadership, it was always more fortunate in appeal. Human slavery more obviously violated democratic institutions than any other evil of the day; it was close enough to irritate and to inflame sensitive minds, yet far enough removed that reformers need have few personal relations with those whose interests were affected. It rasped most severely upon the moral senses of a people whose ideas of sin were comprehended largely in terms of self-indulgence and whose religious doctrines laid emphasis on social usefulness as the proper manifestation of salvation. And, what was more important, slavery was now confined to a section whose economic interests, and hence political attitudes, conflicted sharply with those of the Northeast and upper Northwest.

Almost from the beginning of the new anti-slavery movement, two distinct centers of action appeared, each with its distinct and individual approach to the problem. One developed in the industrial areas of New England. Its most important spokesman was William Lloyd Garrison, founder and editor of a Boston abolition paper called the *Liberator*. Garrison at first accepted the old idea that slavery was an *evil* to be pointed out and gradually eradicated by those among whom it existed, but he shifted his position in the early 1830's and denounced slavery as a damning crime to be unremittingly assailed and immedi-

ately destroyed. The first issue of his paper announced a program from which he never deviated: ". . . *I do not wish to think or speak or write with moderation. I will not retreat a single inch, and I will be heard.*" The problem, as Garrison saw it, was one of abstract right and wrong. The Scriptures and the Declaration of Independence had already settled the issue. Slavery could have no legal status in a Christian democracy. If the Constitution recognized it, then the Constitution should be destroyed. Slaveholders were both sinners and criminals. They could lay no claim to immunity from any mode of attack.

The character of this movement and its leadership is strikingly revealed in an incident related by one of Garrison's traveling companions:

As we rode through the [Franconia] Notch after friends Beach and Rogers, we were alarmed at seeing smoke issue from their chaise-top, and we cried out to them that their chaise was afire! We were more than suspicious that it was something worse than that, and that the smoke came out of friend Rogers' mouth. And so it turned out. This was before we reached the Notch tavern. Alighting there to water our beasts, we gave him, all round a faithful admonition. For anti-slavery does not fail to spend its intervals of public service in mutual and searching correction of the faults of its friends. We gave it soundly to friend Rogers—that he, an abolitionist, on his way to an anti-slavery meeting, should desecrate his anti-slavery mouth . . . with a stupefying weed. We had halted at the Iron Works tavern to refresh our horses, and while they were eating walked to view the Furnace. As we crossed the little bridge, friend Rogers took out another cigar, as if to light it when we should reach the fire! "Is it any malady you have got, brother Rogers," said we to him, "that you smoke that thing, or is it habit and indulgence merely?" "It is nothing but habit," said he gravely; "or I would say, it was nothing else," and he significantly cast the little roll over the railing into the Ammonoosuck.

"A Revolution!" exclaimed Garrison, "a glorious revolution without noise or smoke," and he swung his hat cheerily about his head. It was a pretty incident. . . . It was a vice abandoned, a self indulgence denied, and from principle. It was quietly and beautifully done. . . . Anti-slavery wants her mouths for other uses than to be flues for besotting tobacco-smoke. They may as well almost be rum-ducts as tobacco-funnels. . . . Abolitionists are generally as *crazy* in regard to rum and tobacco as in regard to slavery. Some of them refrain from eating flesh and drinking tea and coffee. Some of them are so bewildered that they want in the way of Christian retaliation . . . they are getting to be monomaniacs, as the Reverend Punchard called us, on *every* subject.

The extreme and impractical nature of the Garrison anti-slavery drive served to attract attention and arouse antagonism rather than to solve the problem. It did, however, show how profoundly the conditions of the time had stirred the reform spirit and how wide the door had been opened to the professional reformers—men to whom the question was not so much "how shall we abolish slavery, as how shall we best discharge our duty . . . to ourselves." Garrison may be taken as typical of the group. His temperament and experiences had combined to set him in most relationships against the accepted order of things. His life would probably have been spent in protesting even if slavery had never existed. From childhood he had waged a bitter fight *against* obstacles and *for* a due recognition of his abilities. A drunken father had abandoned the family to extreme poverty before William was three years old, and the boy, denied all but the rudiments of an education, had first been placed under the care of Deacon Bartlett, and then apprenticed for seven years to one Ephraim Allen to learn the printing trade. His first venture after his apprenticeship was over failed. His second gave him the opportunity to strike back at an unfair world. He became an editor of the *National Philanthropist*, a paper devoted to the suppression of "intemperance and its Kindred vices." This publication served also as a medium through which to attack lotteries, Sabbath-breaking, and war. A new Garrison began to emerge. His personality, given opportunity for expression, asserted itself. Attending a nominating caucus in Boston, he made bold to speak, and, being resented as an upstart, he replied to his critic in a letter to the Boston *Courier:*

It is true my acquaintance in this city is limited. . . . Let me assure him, however, that if my life be spared, my name shall one day be known to the world—at least to such an extent that common inquiry shall be unnecessary.

To another critic he reiterated this statement, adding these significant words: "I speak in the spirit of prophecy, not of vainglory—with a strong pulse, a flashing eye, and a glow of the heart. The task may be yours to write my biography.

Anti-slavery efforts entered the Garrison program when Benjamin Lundy, the pioneer abolitionist, invited him to help edit the *Genius of Universal Emancipation* in Baltimore. Hostile treatment there, climaxed by imprisonment for libel, together with the influence of extreme British opinion, changed a moderate attitude which admitted "that immediate and complete emancipation is not desirable . . . no rational man cherishes so wild a vision," into the extreme and uncompromising fanaticism expressed only two years later in the *Liberator*. From that time on Garrison was bothered only by the fact that the English language was inadequate for the expression of his violent opinions. Southerners in Congress were desperados.

We would sooner trust the honor of the country . . . in the hands of the inmates of our penitentiaries and prisons than in their hands . . . they are the meanest of thieves and the worst of robbers. . . . We do not acknowledge them to be within the pale of Christianity, or republicanism, or humanity!

Hatred of the South had supplanted love for the Negro!

In such an approach as this, there could be no delay, no moderation. Right was right, and wrong was wrong. The Slaveholder could not be spared or given time to learn the evil of his ways. Action immediate and untempered was demanded. . . .

Two principal assumptions stood out in this anti-slavery indictment of the slaveholder. He was, in the first place, the arch-aristocrat. He was the great enemy of democracy. He was un-American, the oppressor of his fellow men, the exploiter of a weaker brother. Against him could be directed all the complaints and fears engendered by industrial captains and land speculators. He, more than any other aristocrat, threatened to destroy the American democratic dream.

In the second place, he was a flagrant sinner. His self-indulgence was un-matched. His licentious conduct with Negro women, his intemperance in the use of intoxicating liquors, his mad dueling, and his passion for war against the weak were enough to mark him as the nation's moral enemy number one! The time for dealing moderately had passed. Immediate reform was imperative.

Thus it was that the slaveholder began to do scapegoat service for all aristocrats and all sinners. To him were transferred resentments and fears born out of local conditions. Because it combined in itself both the moral and the democratic appeal, and because it coincided with sectional rivalry, the abolition movement gradually swallowed up all other reforms. The South became the great object of all efforts to remake American society. Against early indifference and later persecution, a handful of deadly-in-earnest men and women slowly built into a section's consciousness the belief in a Slave Power. To the normal strength of sectional ignorance and distrust they added all the force of Calvinistic morality and American democracy and thereby surrounded every Northern interest and contention with holy sanction and reduced all opposition to abject depravity. When the politician, playing his risky game, linked expansion and slavery, Christian common folk by the thousands, with no great personal urge for reforming, accepted the Abolition attitudes toward both the South and slavery. Civil war was then in the making.

Martin B. Duberman: THE ABOLITIONISTS AND PSYCHOLOGY

One of the country's younger historians, Martin B. Duberman, began his scholarly career in a period when important post-Freudian psychological theories offered new concepts for examining human behavior and when the struggle for Negroes' civil rights encouraged a new imaginative identification with abolitionists. He has turned both these factors to advantage in the following article. Duberman, author of Charles Francis Adams, 1807–1886, *is on the faculty of Princeton University.*

O UT OF their heightened concern with the pressing question of Negro rights, a number of historians, especially the younger ones, have begun to take a new look at the abolitionists, men who in their own day were involved in a similar movement of social change. About both them and ourselves we are asking anew such questions as the proper role of agitation, the underlying motives of both reformers and resistants, and the useful limits of outside interference. From this questioning a general tendency has developed to view the abolitionists in a more favorable light than previously. As yet, however, it is a tendency only, and hostility to the abolitionists continues to be strong among historians.[1]

[1] I deliberately refrain from citing specific works and authors. In suggestions as tentative as mine, I have not thought it profitable to take issue with individuals. I wish to make clear that I am not suggesting that *all* historians have viewed the abolitionists without sympathy or understanding. Men such as Louis Filler, Dwight Dumond, Irving Bartlett, Leon Litwack, Ralph Korngold, Louis Ruchames, Oscar Sherwin, and David Davis have, in varying degrees, and with varying effectiveness, demonstrated their sympathy. But they have

Perhaps one reason why no fuller re-evaluation has taken place is that historians have been made cautious by the fate of previous "revisionist" scholarship. We have seen how current preoccupations can prompt dubious historical re-evaluations. But this need not always be the case. Contemporary pressures, if recognized and contained, can prove fruitful in stimulating the historical imagination. They may lead us to uncover (not invent) aspects of the past to which we were previously blind.

If historians need more courage in their re-consideration of the abolitionists, they also need more information. Particularly do they need to employ some of the insights and raise some of the questions which developments in related fields of knowledge have made possible. Recent trends in psychology seem especially pertinent, though historians have not paid them sufficient attention. It is my hope in this paper to make some beginning in that direction.

not, in my view, as yet carried the majority of historians along with them.

From Martin B. Duberman, "The Abolitionists and Psychology," *The Journal of Negro History,* XLVII (July 1962), pp. 183–91. Reprinted by permission of The Association for the Study of Negro Life and History, Inc.

It might be well to start by referring to one of psychology's older principles, the uniqueness of personality. Each individual, with his own genetic composition and his own life experience, will develop into a distinctive organism. There are, of course, certain universal processes common to the species—that cluster of basic drives and reflexes which are more or less "instinctive." There are also a variety of common responses conditioned by our membership in a particular group, be it family, class, church or nation. These similarities among human beings make possible such disciplines as sociology, anthropology and social psychology, which concern themselves with patterns of behavior, and demonstrate that no man is *sui generis*. But it does not follow that the qualities which are uniquely individual are mere irrelevancies. As Gordon Allport has said, ". . . all of the animals in the world are psychologically less distinct from one another than one man is from other men."[2]

This is not to question, of course, the validity of attempts, whether they be by sociologists, psychologists or historians, to find meaningful similarities in the behavioral patterns of various human groups. The point is to make certain that such similarities genuinely exist, and further, to be aware that in describing them, we do not pretend to be saying *everything* about the individuals involved. Historians, it seems, are prone to ignore both cautions—their treatment of the abolitionists being the immediate case in point.

With barely a redeeming hint of uncertainty, many historians list a group of "similar traits" which are said to characterize all abolitionists: "impractical,"

"self-righteous," "fanatical," "humorless," "vituperative," and,—if they are very modern in their terminology—"disturbed." The list varies, but usually only to include adjectives equally hostile and denunciatory. The stereotype of the "abolitionist personality," though fluid in details, is clear enough in its general outlines.

But did most abolitionists really share these personality traits? The fact is, we know much less about the individuals involved in the movement than has been implied. Some of the major figures, such as Joshua Leavitt, have never received biographical treatment; others—the Tappans, Edmund Quincy, and Benjamin Lundy, for example—badly need modern appraisal. And the careers and personalities of the vast majority of significant secondary figures—people like Lydia Maria Child, Sidney Gay, Maria Weston Chapman, Henry B. Stanton, and Abby Kelley Foster—have been almost totally unexplored. Whence comes the confidence, then, that allows historians to talk of "the abolitionist personality," as if this had been microscopically examined and painstakingly reconstructed?

Certainly the evidence which we do have, does not support such confident theorizing. In order to adhere to this conceptual strait-jacket, it is necessary to ignore or discount much that conflicts with it—the modesty of Theodore Weld, the wit of James Russell Lowell, the tender humanity of Whittier, the worldly charm of Edmund Quincy. This does not mean that we need leap to the opposite extreme and claim all abolitionists were saints and seraphs. But if some of them were disagreeable or disturbed, we want, instead of a blanket indictment, to know which ones and in what ways; we want some recognition of the variety of hu-

[2] Gordon W. Allport, *Becoming, Basic Considerations for a Psychology of Personality*, Clinton, 1960, 23.

man beings who entered the movement.

It seems to me that what too many historians have done is to take William Lloyd Garrison as a personality symbol for the entire movement (at the same time, ironically, that they deny him the commanding leadership which he was once assumed to have had). Fixing on some of the undeniably "neurotic" aspects of his personality (and bolstered, it should be said, by the eccentric psychographs of other abolitionists—a Gerrit Smith say, or a Stephen Foster), they equate these with the personality structures of all the abolitionists, and conclude that the movement was composed solely of "quacks." In doing so, they fail to do justice to the wide spectrum of personality involved; in fact, they do not even do justice to Garrison, for to speak exclusively of *his* oracular and abusive qualities is to ignore the considerable evidence of personal warmth and kindliness.

It may be that when we know more of other abolitionists, we may with equal certainty be able to single out qualities in them which seem palpable symptoms of "disturbance." But let the evidence at least precede the judgment. And let us also show a decent timidity in applying the label "neurotic." Psychiatrists, dealing with a multitude of evidence and bringing to it professional insights, demonstrate more caution in this regard than do untrained historians working with mere traces of personality. If the disposition to be hostile exists, "neurosis" can almost always be established. Under the Freudian microscope, it would be a rare man indeed whose life showed no evidence of pathological behavior. (Think, for one, of the admirable William James, who, as his devoted biographer, Ralph Barton Perry, has shown, was subject to hypochondria, hallucina-

tions, and intense oscillations of mood.) I am not suggesting that all men's lives, if sufficiently investigated, would show equally severe evidence of disturbance. I mean only to warn that, given the double jeopardy of a hostile commentator and the weight of a hostile historical tradition, we must take special precaution not to be too easily convinced by the "evidence" of neurosis in the abolitionists.

And even were we to establish the neurotic component of behavior, the story would certainly not be complete. To know the pathological elements in an individual's behavior is not to know everything about his behavior. To say that Garrison, in his fantasy world, longed to be punished and thus deliberately courted martyrdom, or that Wendell Phillips, alienated from the "new order," sought to work out his private grievances against the industrial system by indirectly attacking it through slavery, is hardly to exhaust the range of their possible motives. We know far too little about why men do anything—let alone why they do something as specific as joining a reform movement—to assert as confidently as historians have, the motives of whole groups of men. We may never know enough about the human psyche to achieve a comprehensive analysis of motivation; how much greater the difficulty when the subject is dead and we are attempting the analysis on the basis of partial and fragmentary remains.

Our best hope for increased understanding in this area—aside from the artist's tool of intuition—is in the researches of psychology. But at present there is no agreed-upon theory of motivation among psychologists. Gordon Allport, however, summarizing current opinion, suggests that behavior does not result solely from the need to reduce tension, but may also aim (especially in a "healthy" person) at distant goals, the achievement of which can be gained only by maintaining tension.[3] Allport does not press his views, realizing the complexity of the problems at issue. But his hypotheses are at least suggestive as regards the abolitionists, for their motives, rather than being solely the primitive ones of eliminating personal tension (under the guise of ethical commitment), may also have included a healthy willingness to bear tension (in the form of ostracism, personal danger and material sacrifice) in order to persevere in the pursuit of long-range ideals.

Acceptance of these suggestions runs into the massive resistance of neo-Freudian cynicism.[4] How old-fashioned, it will be said, to talk in terms of "ideals" or "conscience," since these are only unconscious rationalizations for "darker" drives which we are unable to face. How old-fashioned, too, to talk as if men could exercise choice in their conduct, since all our behavior is determined by our antecedents.

But the surprising fact is that such views are not old-fashioned. On the contrary, they have recently returned to favor in psychoanalytical circles.[5] Increasing dissatisfaction with the ability of behaviorist theory fully to explain human action, has led to a re-consideration of the role of reason and the possibilities of purposive, deliberate behavior. The result is the influential new school of "ego psychology," which views man as endowed with a considerable margin of freedom and responsibility, and which has restored to the vocabulary such "old-fashioned" terminology as character, will-power and conscience. Moral earnestness, moreover, is no longer equated with self-deception. As Allport has said, the very mark of maturity "seems to be the range and extent of one's feeling of self-involvement in abstract ideals."[6] Some of these new emphases had been prefigured in the work of such philosophers as Sartre, who have long stressed social action as a sign of "authenticity" in man.

But although all of this makes a re-evaluation of the abolitionists possible, it does not make one necessary. Men may now be thought capable of impersonal devotion to ideals, but this does not mean that the abolitionists were such men. Maturity may now be defined as the ability to commit ourselves objectively to ethical values, but it does not follow that every man who makes such a commitment does so out of mature motives.

Yet at least some doubts should be raised in our minds as to whether we have been fair in regarding the abolitionists as psychologically homogeneous, and at that, homogeneous in the sense of being self-deceived. My own feeling goes beyond doubt, into conviction. I do not claim, to repeat, that because the abolitionists fought in a noble cause, their motives were necessarily noble—i.e., "pure" and "unselfish," unrelated in any way to their own inner turmoil or conflicts. A connection between inner problems and outer convictions probably always exists to some degree. But an individual's public involvement is never completely explained by discussing his private pathology. Yet it is just this that historians have

[3] Allport, *op. cit.,* 65–68.
[4] Based largely on what people think Freud said, rather than what he actually said. See Philip Rieff, *Freud: The Mind of the Moralist,* N. Y., 1959.
[5] See, for example, O. Hobart Mowrer, "Psychiatry and Religion," *The Atlantic,* July, 1961.

[6] Allport, *op. cit.,* 45.

frequently done, and to that degree, they have distorted and devalued the abolitionist commitment.

To provide a concrete example, by way of summary, consider the case of James Russell Lowell, whose biography I am writing, and about whom I can talk with more assurance than I might some other figure.

His history seems to me convincing proof that at least *some* people became abolitionists not primarily out of an unconscious need to escape from personal problems, but out of a deliberate, rational commitment to certain ethical values—recognizing, as I have said, that the two are never wholly unrelated. Lowell's active life as a reformer came during the period of his greatest contentment—secure in a supremely happy marriage, and confident of his talents and his future. His contemporaries agree in describing him as a gay, witty, warm man, without serious tensions or disabling anxieties. I have come across so little evidence of "pathology" in the Lowell of these years that when the standard picture of the abolitionist as a warped eccentric is applied to him, it becomes absurd.

And he *was* an abolitionist, though various arguments have been used to deny this. Lowell, it has been said, came to the movement late—and only at the instigation of his bride, Maria White, who was a confirmed reformer, never fully committed himself to abolition, and finally left the ranks in the early 1850s. There may be some justice to these charges, but on the whole the argument is not persuasive. Given Lowell's youth (he was born in 1819) he could not have joined the movement much earlier than he did (which was around 1840), and there is evidence that he was involved in the cause before he met Ma-

ria White. The important point is that for roughly ten years he was unquestionably a serious abolitionist, both as an active member of the Massachusetts Anti-Slavery Society, and as a frequent contributor to abolitionist periodicals. The reasons for his drifting out of the movement are complex, but turn largely on the fact that his wife's death in 1853 destroyed the structure of his life and left him apathetic to public issues. (Might not this give added weight to the argument that it takes a reasonably contented man to interest himself in the problems of others?)

Even when it is admitted that Lowell was an abolitionist, he is dismissed as not having been a "typical" one. But who was the typical abolitionist? Is the standard of measurement meant to be some outstanding individual—Garrison, say, or Theodore Weld—and is everyone else to be considered more or less of an abolitionist depending on how closely he approximated the personality structure of the model? But a man may be prominent in a movement without necessarily typifying it. And which of several leading—and very different—figures should be chosen as the model? The decision is likely to be arbitrary (and unconscious), varying with each historian.

Or is the standard of measurement meant to be some composite group of traits which accurately describe the large number of abolitionists, so that when any single individual fails to exhibit these traits, he may justifiably be dismissed as "the exception which proves the rule?"[7] This approach is more reasonable, but here again we run up against the old difficulty of drawing a genuinely valid group portrait. We know so little

[7] It is interesting that in its original form, the aphorism read: "is this the exception which *probes* the rule?"

about the individual personalities and careers of the majority of abolitionists that it seems like putting the cart before the horse to even talk about a composite portrait. Certainly the one which is now commonly accepted ("impractical"; "self-righteous," etc.) fails adequately to describe many of the abolitionists about whom we do have information. I mean here not only Lowell, but a number of others. What I have seen in my researches into the papers of people like Edmund Quincy, Lydia Maria Child or Maria Weston Chapman (to name only a few of the more prominent), has created the strong suspicion in my mind that if their personalities were to be investigated in depth, they too would be found to deviate from the accepted portrait in so many significant ways as further to undermine its reliability.

A conceptual scheme may yet be devised which adequately describes the motives and actions of most of the abolitionists. But if so, it will not be of the primitive kind thus far suggested. There is no reason why historians cannot legitimately investigate group patterns, but to do so meaningfully, they must become skilled in the techniques of sociology and other related disciplines. This takes time and inclination, and the historian, busy with his special interests and orientated towards the particular, rarely has either. Unfortunately this does not always prevent him from trying his hand, though the result has too often

been the elementary kind of categorizing used to describe the abolitionists.

Opinions will continue to differ as to the best way of achieving desired social change. Our own generation's confrontation with segregation has made this clear. Many of us feel as strongly about the evil of that practice as the abolitionists did about the institution of slavery. Like them, too, we have scant faith in Southern voluntarism or the benevolent workings of time; patience and inactivity have not done their work. Naturally we would like to believe that our sense of urgency comes from concern for the Negro rather than from a need to escape from some private torment of our own. Because of this we are admittedly prone to credit our historical counterparts with the kind of "good" motives we would like to impute to ourselves. Our wish to think well of these people may account for our doing so. But as Erich Fromm has said, "the fact that an idea satisfies a wish does not mean necessarily that the idea is false."[8] There is much in the new psychology to encourage the belief that the idea is not false. At any rate, if we are to find out, we need less dogma, more research, and a chastening sense of wonder at the complexities of human nature.

[8] Erich Fromm, *Psychoanalysis and Religion,* Clinton, 1959, 12.

Stanley Elkins: SLAVERY: A PROBLEM IN AMERICAN INSTITUTIONAL AND INTELLECTUAL LIFE

Stanley Elkins is a historian known for his willingness to use the concepts and methods of the social sciences. In a fruitful collaboration, he and Eric McKitrick have produced a series of articles presenting fresh approaches to several areas of American history. The volume from which the following selection is taken applies concepts of sociology, cultural anthropology and social psychology to historical problems concerning slavery and antislavery. This excerpt presents in highly condensed fashion Elkins's theory that abolitionists acted as they did because of the nature of American society, notably its lack of institutions and its exaggeration of the importance of the individual. It would have been better, he contends, if abolitionists had seen slavery as an institution "mutable like others." Elkins teaches history at Smith College.

IT WAS inherent in the state of sensibility which Western civilization had attained by the nineteenth century that slavery, involving the most basic values of humanity, should at that time become morally absorbing to both Europeans and Americans. Englishmen, Frenchmen, Spaniards, and Portuguese each responded to the oppressive subject at various levels of intensity in thought and action; out of their complex experience each could focus upon slavery a variety of resources in order that they might judge its evils, mitigate its abuses, and finally abolish it altogether. There is a certain sense in which the same might be said of the Americans. Yet the simple and harsh moral purity of our own antislavery movement, from the 1830's on, gave it a quality which set it apart from the others. The theory of society which was its backdrop, the intellectual expressions upon which it drew, the slo-

gans which it sent to the market place, the schemes for practical action which it evolved—every phase of the movement combined to produce in our abolitionists that peculiar quality of abstraction which was, and has remained, uniquely American. For them, the question was *all* moral; it must be contemplated in terms untouched by expediency, untarnished by society's organic compromises, uncorrupted even by society itself. It was a problem of conscience which by mid-century would fasten itself in one form or another, and in varying degrees, upon men's feelings everywhere.

But while our thinkers and reformers considered the issue in such abstract purity, in such simple grandeur, there was, in principle if not in fact, an alternative philosophical mode. Slavery might have been approached not as a problem in pure morality but as a question of institutional arrangements—a question of

Reprinted from *Slavery: A Problem in American Institutional and Intellectual Life* by Stanley M. Elkins by permission of The University of Chicago Press, pp. 27–37, 175–78, 183–85, 189–93. © by The University of Chicago, published 1959. For footnotes see the original.

those institutions which make the crucial difference in men's relationships with one another, of those arrangements whereby even so theoretically simple a connection as that between master and slave might take any of a dozen forms among which the sharpest and finest of moral distinctions might be made. This approach was of course never taken, and to expect it of nineteenth-century Americans would be to make impossible demands upon their experience. It is, however, still of interest to ask why this should be so. Why should the American of, say, 1830 have been so insensitive to institutions and their function?

Consider the seeming paradox of how by that time, in the very bright morning of American success, the power of so many American institutions had one by one melted away. The church had fallen into a thousand parts. The shadow of an Anglican church, disestablished in the wake of the Revolution and its doom forever sealed by the yearly anarchy of the camp meeting, was all that remained in the South of vested ecclesiastical authority; and in New England the Congregational church, which had once functioned as a powerful state establishment, was deprived of its last secular supports early in the century. It was not that religion itself was challenged—quite the contrary—but that as a source both of organized social power and internal discipline the church had undergone a relentless process of fragmentation. Religious vitality everywhere was overwhelming, but that vitality lay primarily in demands for individual satisfaction which took inevitable and repeated priority over institutional needs. The very ease with which the great evangelical sects could divide, by a sort of cellular fission, into myriads of tiny independent units, showed that the institutional balance between official coercion and individual self-expression had completely broken down.

As for the bar, the very profusion of lawyers on the American scene, their numbers daily increasing, made a central focus of traditional and vested power among them out of the question; no such continuing structure as the English bar, with its institutional self-awareness, its standards of competence and discipline, its stabilized recruitment, its Temples and Inns of Court, could exist in America. There was a brief period, in the later eighteenth century, when organizations of the bar in our eastern cities did appear capable of providing such a nucleus of stability. But here too, as with the church and the ministry, the great expansion getting under way after the War of 1812, bringing so widespread a demand for services of whatever quality, soon made it clear that individual drives rather than institutional needs would prevail. With the democratization of the bar and its inevitable decline in standards, came a deterioration of whatever institutional bulwarks the bar might have developed.

In our politics, as elsewhere, the old organizational balance was dissolving; something new and unprecedented was emerging in the shape of mass parties. In a way, of course, the sheer formlessness of the new system would cloak an inscrutable logic; its very innocence of principle would foster a special conservatism; its apparent lack of focus would be its own protection, enabling it to act as a kind of super-institution absorbing the functions of a dozen institutions which no longer existed. Yet in its very birth it was necessary that an older, a more stable and traditional conception of political responsibility should disappear. The Federalist party, even in New

England, was by 1830 utterly dead. The Federalists, though in actual policy hardly different from their successors, had assumed and embodied certain traditional attributes of political life which later establishments did not and could not provide. They took their impulse and *esprit* from the Fathers themselves, and their very aura of exclusiveness made possible a certain sharpness of focus. They took for granted the tradition that politics was an occupation for men of affairs, property, and learning. The Federalist party, by its very air of vested interest, came closer than any of its successors to providing a clear institutional nucleus for the loyalty and commitment of other vested interests in society—the intelligentsia, the ministry, the bar, the propertied classes. But the wide democratization of politics in the 1820's ordained that political life in the United States should assume a completely new tone, one quite different from that imagined by the Fathers. Even the Jeffersonians, following the Federalists, had moved more or less instinctively to establish institutional safeguards for political leadership, discipline, and power; yet they too, in the 1820's, saw their special creation, the congressional caucus, swept away and damned as an engine of aristocracy and privilege.

Even in the country's economic activity this breakdown of structural equilibrium was quite as evident as it was in other sectors of public life. The reasonably stable economic organizations maintained by the great trading families of the East were being challenged by a rising class of petty industrialists everywhere. It need not be supposed that these mercantile and banking structures were in a state of decline; yet in a relative sense their power and leadership, amid the proliferation of the small enterprise, no longer carried the decisive weight of former times. The very tone of business life assumed a character peculiarly indicative of what was happening. Its keynote was the individual confronted with boundless opportunity; a veritable new culture-hero was being fashioned on the frontier of the Old Northwest: the young man on the make, in whose folklore the eastern banker, bulwarked by privilege and monopoly, would become a tarnished symbol. The one really effective economic institution that did exist—the second Bank of the United States—was consigned to oblivion amid the cheers of the populace. Capitalism was burgeoning indeed, but in anything but a conservative way; its very dynamism was breaking old molds. Whatever institutional stability American capitalism could conceivably develop was at its lowest possible ebb in 1830.

And yet it was a society whose very energy and resources had themselves become a kind of stability. For such a society, traditional guaranties of order had become superfluous. Its religion was so dynamic that it needed no church; its wealth and opportunity were so boundless that a center of financial power could lose its meaning; and in its need for politicians and lawyers by the thousands it could do without a governing class and ignore many an ancient tradition of bench and bar. Thus for the American of that day it was the very success of his society—of capitalism, of religious liberalism and political democracy—that made it unnecessary for him to be concerned with institutions. Had he a "past"? Yes; it was already two hundred years old, but he could afford to forget it. Had he once known "institutions"? Yes, of a sort, but he could now ignore their meaning; *his* style of life did not depend upon them. His new system of values could now question "society" itself, that very society which had made success possible and which offered him his future. Because he no longer seemed to need it, it became an abstraction which even bore certain allusions to the sinister. He was able to imagine that "stability" resided not in social organization but in "human nature." He no longer appeared to draw from society his traditions, his culture, and all his aspirations; indeed he, the transcendent individual—the new symbol of virtue—now "confronted" society; he challenged it as something of a conspiracy to rob him of his birthright. Miraculously, all society then sprang to his aid in the celebration of that conceit.

We may suppose that such was not merely the general sense but one shared by those men who in other societies would be called "intellectuals"—those men whose traditional preoccupation is to reflect and express in various ways the state of society at large, its tensions, its ills, its well-being. So we should also ask about the consequences which such a happy state of things might have had for intellectual activity. Might there not have been (in spite of everything) a price? Where, for instance, in such a setting were art and learning to find their occupation? "No author, without a trial," wrote the lonely Hawthorne in his preface to *The Marble Faun*, "can conceive the difficulty of writing a romance about a country where there is no shadow, no antiquity, no mystery, no picturesque and gloomy wrong, nor anything but a commonplace prosperity, in broad and simple daylight, as is happily the case with my dear native land." This society with few problems and few visible institutions set the American intellectual, such as he was, peculiarly on his own

and made him as susceptible as anyone else to the philosophy of self-help. In the America of the 1830's and 1840's there was no other symbol of vitality to be found than the individual, and it was to the individual, with all his promise, that the thinker, like everyone else, would inexorably orient himself. Every reward which the age offered seemed pointed out by the way of self-reliance. But the thinker, thus oriented, left himself without a specific and concrete sense of society as such and without even a strong sense of himself as belonging to a community of other men of intellect. He was involuntarily cut off from the sources of power (the political, ecclesiastical, and financial power had become more and more diffuse), so that he could no longer operate, as it were, in the midst of things. For Americans of this generation the very concept of power—its meaning, its responsibilities, its uses—was something quite outside their experience. This intellectual disengagement from problems of power had a great deal to do with the peculiar abstractness of our thought on the subject of slavery.

Such was the state of mind in which Americans faced the gravest social problem that had yet confronted them as an established nation. Theirs had been, considering the bulk of their achievement, a mild existence in which the stimuli of chronic and complex institutional tensions had been absent; it was in such a setting that their habits of thought had been shaped; such was the experience with which they might approach the ills of society and deal with serious questions of morality.

By the 1830's slavery had come to offend the sensibilities of all Christendom. It was a problem partaking of the

Christian conception of sin. Mortal sin lay in the path of all who dealt in slaves, and it was so defined and given meaning by the Christian church in countries where the church had power. Slavery, by its very age, had almost assumed the character of original sin, entailed as it was upon living generations by their predecessors. In America, slavery was unique among the other institutions of society. In one section of the country it had existed for over two centuries, having become interwoven with the means of production, the basic social arrangements, and the very tone of Southern culture. Slavery in the South, instead of diminishing, had spread. Though it had been a source of discomfort there a generation before, men could now see it, under pressure, as the keystone of a style of life in a sense that was not true of any other institution in American society. Conversely, it was at this very time that Americans of the North found themselves suddenly confronted, as it were, with slavery's full enormity.

"No picturesque and gloomy wrong"— Hawthorne here referred to a society which, distinguished from the civilizations of Europe, was not concretely acquainted with sin. The innocence of America and the wickedness of Europe would form one of the great themes of nineteenth-century literature, but of all the writers who used it, perhaps it was Hawthorne's most distinguished biographer, Henry James, who best understood how even "sin," in European culture, had been institutionalized. There, an actual place had been made for it in life's crucial experience. It had been classified from time out of mind and given specific names; the reality of "lust," "avarice," and "oppression" had given rise to the most intricate of social arrangements, not for eliminating them, but for softening their impact and limiting their scope—for protecting the weak and defining the responsibilities of the strong. One powerful social agency in particular had made of iniquity its special province and had dealt with it in a thousand forms for centuries. All this may well have been in James's mind when he exclaimed of America: "*no church.*"

What, then, might be expected to happen if sin *should* suddenly become apparent, in a nation whose every individual was, at least symbolically, expected to stand on his own two feet? The reaction was altogether destructive. The sense of outrage was personal; the sense of *personal* guilt was crushing. The gentle American of mild vices was transformed into the bloody avenger. It would seem that the reaction of a society to sin (as well as to any other problem) depends on the prior experience of that society; whether the wrong shall be torn out root and branch, or whether terms are to be made with it, depends on how intimate that society is with evil in all its forms. The outraged innocent can be a thousand times more terrible than the worldly temporizer. By 1830 the spread of slavery had begun to force upon Americans a catalogue of unsuspected revelations. And accordingly, their guilt and outrage were harassed and quickened from the days of Garrison's first blasts in 1831—"harsh as truth, uncompromising as justice"—until the upheaval of 1861 in which slavery was destroyed with fire and sword.

The sharpest spokesmen of North and South, more and more inclining to stand at polar opposites on all questions touching slavery in the thirty years before the Civil War, had at least a feature of style in common: each expressed himself with a simple moral severity. Each in his way thought of slavery as though it were a gross fact with certain universal, immutable, abstract features unalloyed by considerations of time and place. To the Northern reformer, every other concrete fact concerning slavery was dwarfed by its character as a moral evil—as an obscenity condemned of God and universally offensive to humanity. The Southerner replied in kind; slavery was a positive moral good—a necessary arrangement sanctioned in Scripture and thus by God Himself, in which an inferior race must live under the domination of a superior. "Slavery, authorized by God, permitted by Jesus Christ, sanctioned by the apostles, maintained by good men of all ages, is still existing in a portion of our beloved country." "As a man, a Christian, and a citizen, we believe that slavery is right; that the condition of the slave, as it now exists in slave-holding states, is the best existing organization of civil society." These were characteristic replies to sentiments such as those of the abolitionist George Bourne, who in 1834 had written, "The Mosaic law declares every slaveholder a THIEF; Paul the Apostle classes them among the vilest criminals. . . . To tolerate slavery, or to join in its practice is an insufferable crime, which tarnishes every other good quality. *For whosoever shall keep the law and yet offend in one point, he is guilty of all.*" Neither antagonist, in short—burning with guilt or moral righteousness, as the case may have been—could quite conceive of slavery as a social institution, functioning, for better or worse, by laws and logic like other institutions, mutable like others, a product of human custom, fashioned by the culture in which it flourished, and capable of infinite variation from one culture to another.

There is, in justice, little reason to expect that the question should have been argued otherwise than it was, in view of the intellectual setting available to the pre-Civil War generation. . . .

The anti-institutionalism so characteristic of the Transcendentalists reached heights of extravagance in the speeches and writings of the radical abolitionists. "The difficulty of the present day and with us is," declared Wendell Phillips, "we are bullied by institutions." They attacked the church both North and South as the "refuge and hiding-place" of slavery; the sects—particularly the Methodist—were denounced singly and severally, and Stephen Symonds Foster condemned the entire clergy as a "brotherhood of thieves." Foster also reviled both Whig and Democratic parties for countenancing slavery; Edmund Quincy, Wendell Phillips, and William Lloyd Garrison repudiated the Constitution itself; resolution after resolution was passed in various societies condemning the Union ("No Union with Slaveholders"); and Garrison actually "nominated Jesus Christ to the Presidency of the United States and the World."

No matter [wrote Garrison], though . . . every party should be torn by dissensions, every sect dashed into fragments, the national compact dissolved, the land filled with the horrors of a civil and a servile war—still, slavery must be buried in the grave of infamy, beyond the possibility of a resurrection. If the State cannot survive the anti-slavery agitation, then let the State perish. If the Church must be cast down by the strugglings of Humanity to be free, then let the Church fall, and its fragments be scattered to the four winds of heaven, never more to curse the earth. If the American Union cannot be maintained, except by immolating human freedom on the altar of tyranny, then let the American Union be consumed by a living thunderbolt, and no tear be shed over its ashes. If the Republic must be blotted out from the roll of na-

tions, by proclaiming liberty to the captives, then let the Republic sink beneath
the waves of oblivion, and a shout of joy,
louder than the voice of many waters, fill
the universe at its extinction.

An anti-institutional attitude so pronounced as this could hardly be confined merely to doctrine. It was bound
to have disintegrating effects on the organizational development of the very societies which promoted it. Whereas such
societies did indeed flourish and ex-
pand in the early and middle 1830's,
the truth is that the life of *institutional*
antislavery was doomed to brevity: the
story of abolitionism's spread is not,
after all, that of the strengthening of the
societies as such. On the contrary, the
national organization, after a luminous
but short career, was all but extinguished
during the depression years of the late
thirties and never really recovered. The
story of the movement is to be found
elsewhere.

We have elsewhere noted that the
democratization of all the major institutions once familiar to American life had
to a profound degree worked to undermine those same institutions, and that
in a larger sense such institutional breakdown was the very condition, or price, of
national success. But, in at least one
area, the price of democracy was very
high. For a fatal process was at work,
and that process was nothing less than
the very democratization, North and
South, of the controversy over slavery.
The tragic flaw of an otherwise singularly favored society was the absence of
mechanisms for checking such a development—the absence of mechanisms which
might permit a range of alternatives in
sentiment and idea to be crystallized
and maintained and which might prevent
the development of a lowest common de-

nominator of feeling in each section,
widely enough shared as to provide a
democratic ground for war. . . .

It might well be said that the theme
which dominated the declining phase of
nationally organized abolition activity
was, after all, that of Garrisonian individualism triumphant. Garrison and his methods were peculiarly suited not only to
stamping the movement in his image
and giving it his tone but also to split-
ting the movement's institutional structure. "Garrisonism" was in the last analysis deeply subversive of antislavery's efforts to develop and consolidate organized power. The man himself, with his
egocentric singleness of mind, antago-
nized most of those who tried to combine
with him in any action requiring con-
certed effort. As a result virtually all
such enterprises with which his name
was connected acquired, as Theodore
Weld wrote, a "vague and indefinite
odium." Garrison's own New England
Anti-Slavery Society, which had never
in any case been much concerned with
field operations, split wide apart over
the venom of his attacks on the clergy,
and the movement all over New England fell into disrepute. By the late
thirties the vitality of the American
Anti-Slavery Society itself had been sufficiently sapped by Garrison's reputation that it was quite unable to weather
out the depression years which followed
the 1837 panic. By a touch of irony the
meeting of 1840, at which the society's
final dissolution was to have taken place,
was captured by Garrison with a boat-
load of hastily commissioned "delegates"
brought down from Lynn on an outing.
Nearly all the state auxiliaries promptly withdrew, but this did not disturb
Garrison; he was at last in full control.
Yet the society which he had thus "res-

cued" was by then nothing more than a name.

Garrison's personal legend had been built up at the expense of organized antislavery. It is thus that one may deny his having "represented" in any functioning sense the majority of abolitionists and at the same time exhibit him as the living symbol of abolitionism, so far as the country at large was concerned. He had alienated hundreds by personal contact; his name was deeply distasteful to most middling citizens of the North and anathema to the entire South. But this very fact had made him famous; to think of abolitionism was to think of Garrison. Besides, he had spoken out early; he did have a vocal personal following, and for thousands of local abolitionists who had never seen him and who cared nothing for societies, his name was magic. It was a personal notoriety; he was profoundly the individual, anything but the organizer. As Gilbert Barnes writes, "He was equipped by taste and temperament for free-lance journalism and for nothing else. As a journalist he was brilliant and provocative; as a leader for the antislavery host he was a name, an embodied motto, a figurehead of fanaticism."

"Garrisonism" might thus carry a number of meanings—radical doctrines, intransigence, intolerance, fanaticism—but what is chiefly of interest here is the way it symbolizes the direction in which antislavery, Garrison or no Garrison, was bound to move, even as it spread. That direction was from complexity of doctrine to simplicity, from organization to fragmentation, from consolidated effort to effort dispersed, diffuse and pervasive. Whatever institutional character antislavery might have had, either as colonization or abolition, had broken down

by the 1840's. Nor was this the only institutional breakdown of the period, for it was also in the 1840's that whatever last opportunity there may have been, in the interest of the slave, to exploit the power of the national church organizations disappeared forever. By that time the Methodists and Baptists had quarreled over slavery and split into sectional wings, Northern and Southern.

But while antislavery sentiment and action were thus becoming less and less institutional they were becoming at the same time—almost in inverse ratio—more widely shared. It had been made increasingly clear that the societies conceived their fundamental purpose to be that of spreading the antislavery gospel rather than of striking for the most vulnerable spots in slavery itself. There were now forces at work which made for a diffusion of the issue in such a way that it no longer needed to be carried by the societies; the ground upon which one might conceivably hold antislavery views was being tremendously broadened. The mechanism whereby this was brought about has been denoted in our own time, quite accurately, as the "fellow-traveler" principle.

The process operated somewhat as follows: Relatively few were actually prepared to take unequivocal abolitionist positions, but moral pressures, coming from everywhere in the civilized world and reflected intensely from our own abolitionists, were more and more insistent that Northerners recognize in some form the evils of slavery. Functional substitutes for abolitionism, that is, were coming increasingly into demand. And this growing need for some satisfactory mode of self-expression was in fact being provided for by the appearance of other issues and other forms of action—in some cases broader, and in all cases more acceptable—to which abolitionism could be linked but in which more and more persons could participate. . . .

Finally, the broadest of all such issues, emerging after the Mexican War, was that of "free soil"—an antislavery position so widely shared that by 1860 it could command political majorities in every Northern state but one. It was with this issue that the democratization of antislavery had become complete.

The remainder of our paradigm of antislavery thought with its four explanatory categories—anti-institutionalism, individualism, abstraction, and guilt—is speedily traversed. Various implications of the first of these, anti-institutionalism, have already been noted, and in the process certain things have been said of its counterpart, individualism. As more and more individuals entered the antislavery movement at one level or another, the movement became less and less institutional in character; moreover, between institutional solidarity on the one hand and individual satisfaction and self-expression on the other, the balance would invariably swing to the latter.

Now this very individualism also penetrated, in spite of itself, to the debate over the slave. That debate, focusing as it did upon the Negro's "nature" and "innate capacities," in effect bypassed the nature of the institution within which he acted out his daily life. "The negro is a child in his nature," an anonymous Southerner had written in 1836, "and the white man is to him as a father." He was cheerful and gay, a trait which John Pendleton Kennedy called "constitutional and perennial"; he was imitative and adaptable ("The African adapts himself with greater readiness to circumstances than the white man"), docile and lacking in pride and courage: "The slave, besotted, servile, accustomed to

degradation, and habituated to regard his master with deference and awe, does not presume to dream of contending with him." He was lazy and dishonest: "All history proves that idleness and vice is the only liberty the African aspires to, either in his own country or as a slave in Christian lands." He was irresponsible ("the most improvident race in the world, and must have a superior mind to guide them"), and yet in the last analysis affectionate and loyal. "They look up to their liberal and generous masters, and their mistresses, with a feeling absolutely fond and filial." Slavery, in short, was really the only state in which such a creature could exist. "He is happier . . . as a slave," wrote the Southerner of *The South Vindicated,* "than he could be as a freeman. This is the result of the peculiarities of his character."

The Northern reformer accepted the argument on the Southerner's terms by reversing it, and attempted to refute it with that logic of individual perfectibility upon which the humanitarianism of the day drew so deeply. Lydia Maria Child admitted the existence of ignorance among the Negroes, but insisted that their desire to be otherwise would increase "just in proportion as they are free. The fault is in their *unnatural* situation, not in themselves." Mrs. Child, pointing to the existence of numerous merchants, priests, and doctors in Brazil who had once been slaves, drew the inference not that this was due to institutional differences between American and Brazilian slavery but rather that it was simply freedom which had made the difference. She thought that freedom, followed by universal education, was the remedy and that it was only prejudice that prevented "the improvement of a large portion of the human race." Emancipation, according to William

Jay, would have instant salutary effects upon the Negroes; it would "stimulate their morals, quicken their intelligence, and convert a dangerous, idle, and vicious population into wholesome citizens." The transition from slave to free labor might, he thought, be "effected instantaneously, and with scarcely any perceptible interruption of the ordinary pursuits of life." S. B. Treadwell wrote:

If all the slaves in the United States should have their shackles knocked off, and endowed with the privileges of freemen tomorrow, and barely paid a fair compensation for their labour, (which would also be far better for their masters) they would at once be as capable, from the honest avails of their labour of supporting themselves and their families, in their accustomed mode of living, as any class of people in the world. Of this there can be no question.

It was, and is, perfectly possible to accept both the descriptive accuracy of what the Southerner saw and the attainability, in theory, of what the Northerner hoped for. But not at the level of "the individual and his innate capacities"; to argue it out at that level (innate racial inferiority versus innate human perfectibility) was not only to freeze all hope of mutual understanding but actually to rule out of the argument a formidable social institution. Here was the ante-bellum form of a now-venerable debate—the debate over "Sambo." Finally, the controversy, never very concrete, was raised to empyrean heights of abstraction as both sides resorted to Bible criticism. Each searched the sacred texts, one to show slavery as "consistent with the precepts of patriarchs, apostles, and prophets," the other to prove "The Book and Slavery Irreconcilable," and of course each found the appropriate passages.

What it came down to, after all, was a problem of morality whose intellectual content had become more and more attenuated. It was really the abolitionist, with guilt as both powerful stimulus and powerful weapon, who understood most surely—if only by instinct—the means which would carry the issue furthest. Alternately he writhed and thundered. "My brother," wrote Weld with quiet intensity to James G. Birney,

God's terrors have begun to blaze upon the guilty nation. If repentance, speedy, deep and *national* do[es] not forestall Jehovah's judgments, they will break upon us from the thickening air and the heaving earth and the voice of a brothers blood crying from the ground will peal against the wrathful heavens and shake down ruin as a fig tree casteth her untimely fruit. May God purify us, gird us for the conflict, give us faith and then we shall stand unscathed by the flames which blaze around us.

"How ought I to feel and speak?" Garrison demanded meanwhile, in apocalyptic accents.

My soul should be, as it is, on fire. I should thunder—I should lighten. I should blow the trumpet of alarm, long and loud. I should use just such language as is most descriptive of the crime. I should imitate the example of Christ, who, when he had to do with people of like manners, called them sharply by their proper names—such as, an adulterous and perverse generation, a brood of vipers, hypocrites, children of the devil, who could not escape the damnation of hell.

The Southerner of course, whose own moral tradition was not so very different from Weld's and Garrison's, also writhed. "If you would reform the Southern man," protested Joseph Stiles, "say, if you please, that his explanations do not entirely satisfy you; but say something of them; give them some regard, some weight. For he knows, and so do you, that his views and feelings are such as an intelligent and honest man may well entertain." But the Southerner's guilt could do little other than turn defensive. Nehemiah Adams, a Northern minister who returned from a Southern visit with greatly modified views on Southern morals, had conversed with a slaveholder "of liberal education and great influence at the south, and withal an

extreme defender of the system of slavery." Adams was much impressed by this man's words: "If the north had directed its strength against the evils of slavery instead of assailing it as a sin *per se*, it could not have survived to the present day." While doubtless not worth much as *post hoc* prediction, the statement is an admirable little map of what had happened to Southern squeamishness on the subject of slavery.

Suggestions for Additional Reading

The student should not expect to find a single satisfactory survey of the anti-slavery movement. Older studies, such as Albert B. Hart, *Slavery and Abolition, 1831-1841*, (New York, 1906) and Jesse Macy, *The Anti-Slavery Crusade* (New Haven, 1919), are at best too simple. Two recent histories based on prodigious research are Louis Filler, *The Crusade against Slavery* (New York, 1960) and Dwight L. Dumond, *Antislavery: The Crusade for Freedom in America* (Ann Arbor, 1961), but sheer inclusiveness makes them tough going for newcomers to the field.

Russel B. Nye, *William Lloyd Garrison and the Humanitarian Reformers* (Boston and Toronto, 1955), not primarily biographical, is brief, balanced, and readable. For heartier fare, see Gilbert H. Barnes, *The Antislavery Impulse, 1830-1844* (New York, 1933), a work justly famous for its rediscovery of the importance of non-Garrisonian elements in the movement. The Dumond volume represented in these readings is similar in emphasis. The story of the colonizationists is found in P. J. Staudenraus, *The African Colonization Movement, 1816-1865* (New York, 1961), which supersedes earlier investigations of its subject.

To approach abolitionism through the lives of individual participants the student can consult such reminiscences as Thomas Wentworth Higginson, *Cheerful Yesterdays* (Boston and New York, 1898), and the same author's *Contemporaries* (Boston and New York, 1899); Samuel J. May, *Some Recollections of Our Antislavery Conflict* (Boston, 1869); and Parker Pillsbury, *Acts of the Anti-Slavery Apostles* (Concord, New Hampshire, 1883). Each year, however, sees the appearance of new scholarly biographies of abolitionists, such as Benjamin P. Thomas, *Theodore Weld: Crusader for Freedom* (New Brunswick, New Jersey, 1950); Betty Fladeland, *James Gillespie Birney: Slaveholder to Abolitionist* (Ithaca, 1955); Merton L. Dillon, *Elijah P. Lovejoy: Abolitionist Editor* (Urbana, 1961); Irving H. Bartlett, *Wendell Phillips: Brahmin Radical* (Boston, 1961); John L. Thomas, *The Liberator: William Lloyd Garrison* (Boston and Toronto, 1963); and Walter M. Merrill, *Against Wind and Tide: A Biography of Wm. Lloyd Garrison* (Cambridge, Mass., 1963). This list could easily be extended with meritorious works on less important figures. A stimulating essay that presents a "type" abolitionist leader for the 1830s is David Donald, "Toward a Reconsideration of Abolitionists," in *Lincoln Reconsidered: Essays on the Civil War Era* (New York, 1956).

Those pursuing the case of John Brown will find Oswald Garrison Villard, *John Brown, 1800-1859: A Biography Fifty Years After* (Boston and New York, 1910), the fullest of the biographies and Louis Ruchames, *A John Brown Reader* (London and New York, 1959), a helpful source collection. Both these works are sympathetic to Brown. For more negative interpretations, see James C. Malin, *John Brown and the Legend of Fifty-Six* (Philadelphia, 1942), Robert Penn Warren, *John Brown: The Making of a Martyr* (New York, 1929), and C. Vann Woodward, "John Brown's Private War," in *The Burden of Southern History* (Baton Rouge, 1960). The biography of an abolitionist who aided Brown, Ralph V. Harlow, *Gerrit Smith: Philanthropist and Reformer* (New York, 1939), presents a figure fascinating in his own right.

To see abolitionism in the context of American reformism no other single work is so useful as Alice Felt Tyler, *Freedom's Ferment: Phases of American Social History from the Colonial Period to the Outbreak of the Civil War* (Minneapolis, 1944). The revivalistic evangelicalism that inspired many leaders of the movement can be understood through such works as Charles C. Cole, Jr., *The Social Ideas of the Northern Evangelists, 1826-1860* (New York, 1954) and Timothy L. Smith, *Revivalism and Social Reform in Mid-Nineteenth-Century America* (Nashville, 1957). For an example of the economic environment that hampered antislavery forces, see Philip S. Foner, *Business & Slavery: The New York Merchants & the Irrepressible Conflict* (Chapel Hill, 1941). For the emergence of antislavery as a political issue, three biographies, Samuel Flagg Bemis, *John Quincy Adams and the Union* (New York, 1956); David Donald, *Charles Sumner and the Coming of the Civil War* (New York, 1960); and Frank Otto Gatell, *John Gorham Palfrey and the New England Conscience* (Cambridge, Mass., 1963), are particularly revealing; an older work, Theodore C. Smith, *The Liberty and Free Soil Parties in the Northwest* (New York, 1897), also merits consultation. For the fourteen years preceding the Civil War, Allan Nevins, *Ordeal of the Union* and *The Emergence of Lincoln* (4 vols., New York, 1947-1950), provide both a unique breadth of social and political history and important reinterpretations of such matters as John Brown's Raid.

For a thorough and judicious study of the institution abolitionists were attacking, see Kenneth M. Stampp, *The Peculiar Institution: Slavery in the Ante-Bellum South* (New York, 1956). The best history of the Negro in America is John Hope Franklin, *From Slavery to Freedom: A History of American Negroes* (rev. ed., New York, 1963). Racial attitudes of abolitionists and activities of Negro abolitionists can be traced in Leon F. Litwack, *North of Slavery: The Negro in the Free States, 1790-1860* (Chicago, 1961).

Two works, William S. Jenkins, *Pro-Slavery Thought in the Old South* (Chapel Hill, 1935), and Clement Eaton, *Freedom of Thought in the Old South* (Durham, 1940), complement each other in indicating Southern reactions to abolitionism. For a convenient collection of documents, see Eric L. McKitrick (ed.), *Slavery Defended: The Views of the Old South* (Englewood Cliffs, New Jersey, 1963).

To follow some of the intriguing avenues of comparative history, the student can learn of attacks on slavery in other countries in such works as Frank Tannenbaum, *Slave and Citizen: The Negro in the Americas* (New York, 1947); Frank J. Klingberg, *The Anti-Slavery Movement in England: A Study of English Humanitarianism* (New Haven, 1926); William L. Mathieson, *British Slavery and Its Abolition, 1823-1838* (London, 1926); and Eric Williams, *Capitalism & Slavery* (Chapel Hill, 1944).

Particular aspects of the antislavery movement are treated in Russel B. Nye, *Fettered Freedom: Civil Liberties and the Slavery Controversy, 1830-1860* (East Lansing, 1949), and—especially useful in showing how much legend has become mixed with abolitionist history—Larry

Gara, *The Liberty Line: The Legend of the Underground Railroad* (Lexington, Kentucky, 1961).

The flavor of the abolitionist movement is best captured by reading contemporary documents. An excellent starting place is Louis Ruchames (ed.), *The Abolitionists: A Collection of Their Writings* (New York, 1963). For an understanding of abolitionists through their correspondence, see Gilbert H. Barnes and Dwight L. Dumond (eds.), *Letters of Theodore Dwight Weld, Angelina Grimké Weld, and Sarah Grimké, 1822-1844* (2 vols., New York, 1934), and Dumond (ed.), *Letters of James Gillespie Birney, 1831-1857* (2 vols., New York, 1938). The four volumes of Wendell Phillips Garrison and Francis Jackson Garrison, *William Lloyd Garrison, 1805-1879: The Story of His Life Told by His Children* (New York, 1885-1889), contain many letters and other writings by their subject.

In many libraries the student can at least sample annual reports of the various antislavery societies and such newspapers as the *Liberator*, the *Emancipator*, the *Philanthropist*, the *National Anti-Slavery Standard*, or the *Friend of Man*. Of the many abolitionist descriptions of the peculiar institution, the classic is Theodore D. Weld, *Slavery As It Is: Testimony of a Thousand Witnesses* (New York, 1839).